LEARNING TAROT SPREADS

OTHER BOOKS BY JOAN BUNNING

Learning the Tarot
Tarot Card Combinations (with Dorothy Kelly)
Learning Tarot Reversals

LEARNING
TAROT
SPREADS

Joan Bunning

WEISERBOOKS
San Francisco, CA / Newburyport, MA

To David and Jonathan

First published in 2007 by
Red Wheel/Weiser, LLC
With offices at:
500 Third Street, Suite 230
San Francisco, CA 94107
www.redwheelweiser.com

ISBN 10: 1-57863-270-6
ISBN 13: 978-1-57863-270-1
Library of Congress Cataloging-in-Publication Data available upon request

Cover and book design by Kathryn Sky-Peck
Typeset in Centaur
Printed in the United States of America
MG
10 9 8 7 6 5 4 3 2 1
The paper used in this publication meets the minimum requirements of the
American National Standard for Information Sciences—Permanence of Paper
for Printed Library Materials Z39.48-1992 (R1997).

CONTENTS

ACKNOWLEDGMENTS

I want to thank my family and friends near and far for their steady love and support, especially my husband Steve and children Jonathan and David.

I'm also grateful for all the myriad gifts brought to this project by the staff at Red Wheel/Weiser. In particular, I'd like to thank Caroline Pincus, Jordan Overby, Kathyrn Sky-Peck, Rachel Leach, and Laurie Trufant for their hard work, patience, and good humor every step of the way. You make the process a pleasure.

Finally, I'm deeply grateful to all those who honor the inner life. Just knowing you are "out there"—seeking as I am—has sustained and inspired me more than I can say.

PREFACE

Imagine standing on a train track with a train approaching in the distance. This train is "your future." From your perspective, all you can see is the engine bearing down. The only information you have is what is directly in front of you.

But now imagine rising up and looking in all directions. You can see where the train has come from and where it's going. You can pick out the path you took to the track and see others as well. You have much more knowledge about the total situation.

A tarot reading is one way to rise above the track of your life so you can see forward and backward at the same time. Your present moment is no longer a limited view at track level; it becomes all-encompassing.

How does a reading do this? It opens a line of communication with a part of you that exists at a higher level—your inner guide. Your inner guide knows you very well. It understands why you're standing where you are in the path of an approaching train. When you can contact your inner guide, you enjoy the benefits of both perspectives at the same time.

As you turn more and more to your inner guide, these two views will gradually merge. You'll start seeing your life in a more expansive way. You'll notice the many options available to you and how they connect. With this greater awareness, you can decide where you choose to be at any moment. May you find your cards ever useful as you walk the rails!

INTRODUCTION

Welcome to *Learning Tarot Spreads*—the third book in my series about the tarot. In this book, I talk about spreads—the patterns we use to lay out cards for a reading.

This book is designed for students who are familiar with tarot basics. If you're completely new to the tarot, I recommend starting with my first book, *Learning the Tarot*, or some other beginner's book. Once you know the fundamentals, you'll be able to put the concepts in this book to good use.

To me, the tarot is a tool for personal growth and understanding, so this book is oriented toward readings you do for yourself. The lessons focus on personal readings, but I do talk about how to do readings for others in lesson 12.

Most books about spreads are a cookbook of samples. They offer a variety of layouts to explore, but don't go into much depth about each one. In *Learning Tarot Spreads*, I take a different approach. I want to help you understand spreads more completely. What features do they have in common? Which ones are best for certain subjects? What makes a spread successful? There's so much to discover about these patterns.

Part 1 of *Learning Tarot Spreads* is made up of twelve lessons with accompanying exercises. Lessons 1 through 4 cover spreads in general. Lessons 5 through 12 describe what I call the flex spread—a new way of working with the cards. The flex spread is not a typical spread, but an all-purpose spread "framework"—a method for creating layouts of different kinds. It provides a set of core principles that you can apply to any reading situation. Part 2 contains additional material about spread positions with sample layouts of many kinds. I hope you find this information useful and fun.

PART I

LESSONS

AND

EXERCISES

LESSON 1
THE SPREAD

Our lives have two dimensions—the outer, based in the physical, and the inner, based in spirit. A tarot reading is a way to connect these two worlds. The cards exist in the physical, but they're also portals to the inner dimension, conveying meanings that exist on this deeper level.

When you do a reading, you show faith in life's meaning. You demonstrate your intent to know your world more completely. You consciously open yourself to the inner realm so its messages can be revealed.

What a wonderful and mysterious process! How can you best encourage it? How can you approach a tarot reading so the cards communicate their messages? In these lessons, we'll explore these questions.

Structure and Freedom

There's a tension between structure and freedom in many areas of the tarot. Should card meanings be fixed or fluid? Should a reading be formal or casual? Are rituals required? Readers often debate these questions about the best way to carry out a reading.

At a minimum, there must be a plan for selecting and examining the cards. This can be as simple as picking a few cards at random, or it can involve elaborate preparations and procedures. Most readers prefer an approach somewhere in the middle. They like having a procedure to follow, but not one that's too restrictive. They want to be free to improvise, but not in a vacuum. They just need a framework to guide and direct their intuition. This is the purpose of the tarot spread.

The Spread

A tarot spread is a predefined template or pattern that defines how to distribute and interpret the cards in a reading. A spread limits the scope of a reading for greater focus and clarity. It gives you a predictable way to enhance your intuition without stifling it. It adds structure to the otherwise free flow of a reading.

The basic unit of a spread is the position—a placeholder for one card. Figure 1 below shows a typical three-card spread pattern. The rectangles represent the three positions and their relationship. Figure 2 shows this spread as it might appear after cards have been drawn.

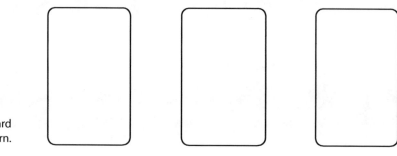

Figure 1. A 3-card spread pattern.

Figure 2. The 3-card spread with cards drawn.

A spread is defined in four ways by its positions: total number, order of placement, location (spread shape), and meanings. Let's take a look at each in turn.

Number of Positions

A spread can have from one to seventy-eight positions—the number of cards in a standard tarot deck. Spreads can be divided roughly into three groups by size:

Small spreads—1-4 positions

Small spreads are easy to learn and use. They convey concise information directly. They're useful when you need a few basic insights quickly.

Medium spreads—5-19 positions

Medium spreads are quite varied. They take longer to learn and interpret, but they offer more detail. They're useful for looking at a single subject in depth.

Large spreads—20+ positions

Large spreads are not as useful as you might think. They can be unwieldy and difficult to grasp as a whole. Also, having so many cards tends to water down the value of each one. Still, large spreads can be revealing if carefully structured. They offer grand vistas you can study over time.

Order of Placement

It's impossible to place every card in a spread at the same time, so an order of placement is necessary. In figure 3, card #1 would be placed first, card #2 would be second, and card #3 third. Placement order is important because meaning grows as cards appear. Your impression of a reading develops as each new card is drawn.

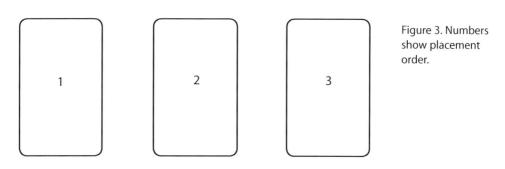

Figure 3. Numbers show placement order.

The first position is key. Card #1 is the opening chord of a symphony. It sets the tone, especially when it's isolated or in the center. The positions that follow build up the body of a spread. The last card often shows an outcome or result, summing up the earlier cards.

Spread Shape

The shape of a spread is determined by the relationship of its positions. In theory, a spread can take any shape, but most have a recognizable design such as a line, a triangle, or a circle. These shapes can also appear within a spread as subgroups of cards. In lesson 3, we'll discuss spread shapes in more detail.

Position Meanings

Each position in a spread has its own individual meaning assigned when the spread is created. This is arguably the most important—and most fascinating—aspect of any spread. In the next lesson, we'll look at how position and card meanings interact to deepen the message of a reading.

Structure and Freedom

Spend some time thinking about structure and freedom. Become aware of the interplay of these two energies in your life. As you go about your affairs, notice what you and others do to create structure or freedom. Consider these questions:

- What is the purpose of structure?
- When do people value structure, and when freedom?
- How does it feel when there's too much of either?
- How much structure do I need in my life?
- Does my preference change with circumstances?

How many positions?

1. Take your tarot deck in your hand. Turn over the top card and place it face up anywhere in front of you. Note the card and its meaning to you.

2. Turn over the next card, and place it in any random spot. Note the meaning of this card and its relation to the first. Continue in this way, trying to keep all the cards vividly connected in your mind.

3. Watch your comfort level as you go. Keeping mental track of a few cards is easy, but it gets harder as you continue. At some point, did you start losing your "grasp" of all the cards?

4. Repeat the exercise, but this time, put the cards into some kind of order as you go. Use any guiding principle—for instance, organizing by number or suit. Notice how this practice eases the way and aids understanding. How many cards can you place when there is structure?

Order of Placement

1. Choose a large spread to work with from the Spread Shapes section (see pages 158–160).

2. Using your tarot deck, recreate the pattern of your chosen spread as quickly as possible. Place the cards in front of you in whatever order occurs to you spontaneously. Don't worry about the cards or their meanings. Do this before reading on.

3. Think about the order you used when placing your cards. What guided your choices? Were you aware of those principles at the time? Did you start on one side or in the middle? Did you go clockwise or counterclockwise? How did you handle opposite positions? Your choices reflect your natural order preferences.

4. Repeat this exercise with a different shape. Be sure to place cards quickly to bypass your conscious mind.

LESSON 2
POSITION MEANINGS

Imagine showing a picture of yourself to a friend. You're smiling in the picture, but there's no clue as to why. Now imagine showing your friend the same picture, but this time in a frame labeled "My first day at work." Suddenly, the picture takes on new meaning. Your friend now knows why you're smiling. The label tells her how to interpret your mood.

In a tarot spread, positions act like labeled frames. A frame is a holder with an empty place for a picture. A position is a holder with an empty place for a card. The meaning of each position comes from its "label." This meaning affects whatever card falls in that position during a reading. It provides a context for the card—a frame of reference.

The Ace of Cups can symbolize love. In a position labeled "What I desire," the Ace of Cups implies a desire for love. In a position labeled "What I fear," this same card shows the opposite—a fear of love. In both cases, the card meaning is the same, but the implication is different. In a frame labeled "My *last* day at work," your smile takes on a whole new meaning!

Positions are the building blocks of spreads. Each position/card combination creates a unique message that blends their meanings. These messages, in turn, combine to form the meaning of a spread as a whole.

Popular Spread Positions

Traditionally, the positions in a spread are defined by its creator. During my research for this book, I explored hundreds of spreads designed by many card readers. I saw unique and unusual positions, but also many repetitions. Gradually, I began to think of positions as having a life of their own, independent of any spread. I realized it would be possible to study them individually, just as we do tarot cards. I decided to keep track of popular positions and work up a detailed definition for each.

The result is the Position Reference on page 73—a collection of twenty-eight positions for use in spreads. Each position has a name, description, keywords, and interpretation hints. The positions are divided into two main groups—subjects and qualities.

Subject Positions

Subjects are people, situations, and other topics of interest in tarot readings. In the reference section, there are three positions used to represent different kinds of subjects in a reading—main, related, and potential. Each one has the same basic meaning. It stands for a subject's central or key issue. In my research, I found this type of position to be the most popular by far. It goes by many names, such as heart of the matter, essence, and main theme. It's found in nearly all spreads because it's so useful. We always want to know what is most essential about ourselves, other people, and situations.

Quality Positions

Quality positions describe the status or condition of a subject. Most are defined in opposite pairs with each position representing one side of a quality. For example, the enduring and temporary positions go together. They are opposites in length of time. In the enduring position, the Hermit suggests solitude is long lasting; in temporary, that it's short-term.

In our dualistic world, whenever we name a certain quality, we always imply its opposite. Hot implies cold. Dark suggests light. This pattern is true for tarot cards,[1] so it makes sense that it's true for positions as well.

There are two positions in the quality group that are not paired. The environment position describes the atmosphere around a subject. It shows what is *other* than the subject. The potential quality position identifies a quality as yet unexpressed.

Guidance Position

The guidance position is unique. The subject and quality positions are what I call "factors." A factor position tells you what is true and real at the time of a reading. It's objective in that it describes how something is, for better or worse. The guidance position is more subjective. It offers personal commentary—a point of view

---

1 See lesson 15 in *Learning the Tarot* for more about opposites within tarot cards.

or way of looking at what's involved. I expand on the difference between factors and guidance in lesson 8.

The Position Reference is a foundation for you to build on. Some positions may be familiar from spreads you use now. Others may be new. Feel free to adjust this collection to suit your personal tarot style. For now, though, the positions in the Reference give us a common language to use throughout this book. I'll refer to them often in the lessons to come.

EXERCISES:

LESSON 2

Position Reference Study

1. Take a few moments to become familiar with the Position Reference. There are entries for subject, quality, and guidance positions.

2. Choose one quality position to examine in detail. Read through the description of your position and its keywords. Note the opposite position if there is one, and read its description as well. Think about how the two positions reflect opposing views. Ignore the flex-spread entry for now.

3. Glance briefly through the accompanying table. This material will become more meaningful later. Right now, your goal is simply to get an overview of what's available for each position. You don't need to study or memorize anything in depth.

Positions in Your Favorite Spreads

Think about the positions in a spread you use now, or one from a tarot book. Compare the positions in your spread with those in the Position Reference. Are any similar? How close are the meanings? What are the differences? My matches for the Celtic Cross spread are in Appendix A (see page 161). Use this exercise to help you begin customizing the reference section to your own tarot practice.

LESSON 3
SPREAD SHAPES

A tarot spread has two levels of meaning. The first comes from the individual positions, as we learned in the last lesson. The second comes from the overall design of the spread. In this lesson, we'll take a look at these spread shapes.

A spread's shape comes from the arrangement of its positions. If the spread's shape is familiar, it's easy to learn and remember. If the positions are random, the spread makes little sense. Structure conveys order and meaning.

Design Principles

Most spread patterns follow four design principles: symmetry, spacing, repetition, and orientation.

Symmetry:

Symmetry is balance among parts. Most spreads use symmetry for beauty and harmony. Positions often mirror each other. Even-numbered spreads tend to be solid and regular—every position has its counterpart. Odd-numbered spreads are more dynamic—the lone position creates tension.

Spacing:

The space between positions is usually uniform. The exception is the use of a wider margin to define a lone position or group of positions. In figure 4 on page 16 the single position in the center is set off by the extra space around it.

Repetition:

Positions are often repeated for balance and uniformity. A spread about two people may have two duplicate sets of cards—one for each person. In figure 4 the 3-card groups to each side are duplicates.

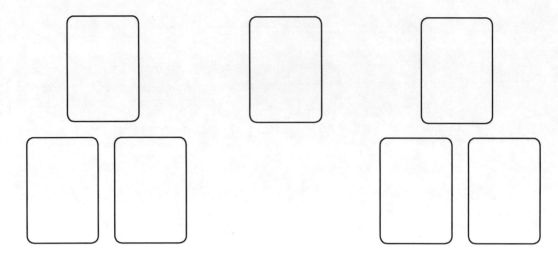

Figure 4. Spacing helps define position groups.

Orientation:

The orientation of a card shows whether it's upright or reversed. In a vertical position, a card's orientation is obvious. If a position is angled or horizontal, the situation is not so clear.[2] You must decide beforehand how to interpret these cases. Any
decision is fine as long as you're consistent from reading to reading.

Spread Patterns

Sacred geometry is the "art of using geometric forms as a gateway to the knowledge and presence of the living spirit."[3] Certain archetypal patterns have the
ability, in and of themselves, to open us to deeper levels. A spread in one of
these shapes resonates with the universal meaning of that form. Below are some
common shapes and their meanings. Each is a spread pattern in its own right, but
also a possible element within a larger layout.

---

2 An example is position 2 of the Celtic Cross spread. See page 279 of *Learning the Tarot*.
3 John Michael Greer, *Techniques for Geometric Transformation* (St. Paul, MN: Llewellyn Publications, 2002),
page 4. This book is the manual for Greer's Sacred Geometry Oracle.

Single:

A solitary position announces "I'm special." In the center of a spread, it shows central importance—a hub of interest. To the side, it shows a unique stance. A single can be at the end of a line to show where all the other positions are leading. It can also be a bridge between two position groups, as in figure 4.

Pair:

A pair consists of two positions that belong together. They can be horizontal, vertical, diagonal, or crossed. A pair creates a two-sided dynamic. It shows two similar or opposing qualities. Position pairs are always interpreted in relation to each other.

Line:

A line is three or more cards in a row—horizontal, vertical, or diagonal. A line can mean "interpret us as a group"—all the positions in the line refer to the same subject. Sometimes a line shows direction, such as the flow of time. In this case, cards for the past are traditionally placed on the left, cards for the present in the center, and cards for the future on the right. Arrows are lines that highlight direction (page 158). A line can also show cause (left) moving toward effect (right). The horseshoe is a line bent into a curve (page 158). It can show the rise and fall of energies or the impact of two influences meeting in the center.

Cross:

A cross is made up of two perpendicular lines. The simplest form has positions in the four directions: north, south, east, and west, with a fifth position in the center as a point of integration (see Greek Cross on page 156). A cross can be extended in any direction with extra positions. The arms of a cross can be the same length or different lengths (see Roman Cross on page 157). The "T" and "L" shapes are variations of the cross lacking one or more arms.

Grid:

A grid is a set of lines grouped together in a square or rectangle. Usually, each line is defined as a unit with the meaning of each position fixed by its row and column. The spread in figure 5 on the next page compares three people over time. The middle position shows "mom" in the "present." The lower right position shows "dad"

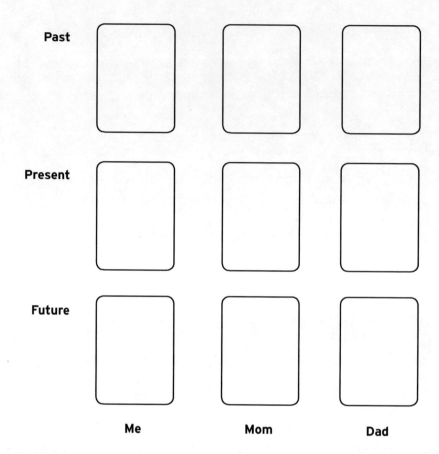

Figure 5. A three-by-three grid spread.

in the "future." Grid spreads are quite versatile. You can create many variations by changing the line definitions.

Triangle:

A triangle is a group of three positions. One simple type has two cards on the bottom and one on top. The two "combine" to create the third, which is their sum or integration.[4] Another triangle has one position on the bottom and two on top. This

---

4 Philosopher Georg Hegel described this relationship as a single thesis contradicted by its antithesis leading to synthesis at a higher level.

shape shows two developments arising from the same root (page 154). The "V" shape is an extension with extra positions. The pyramid is an expanded triangle with additional lines. Each line has one more position than the line before (page 157).

Circle:

A circle suggests unity. In a circular spread, all the positions belong together. They are elements of one whole. The signs of the zodiac and months of the year are often placed in a circle spread. Sometimes, positions in a circle show the many qualities of a subject whose essence is shown by a single in the center (page 158).

Bridge:

A bridge is a single position or line connecting two other lines or groups. Some examples are the "H," "I," and "A" shapes. A bridge literally *bridges* two entities. It shows what joins them or brings them together. The single in figure 4 is a bridge.

EXERCISES:

LESSON 3

Shape Awareness

Many activity books for young children involve finding shapes in pictures. You have to look for the hidden circles and squares on each page. For a day or two, adopt this same shape awareness. Look for geometric figures in your environment. Pay attention to the patterns in material objects, but also to their influence in the abstract. How does it feel when people are in pairs, lines, circles, or triangles? When are bridges in effect? Try to get in touch with the archetypal energies of different shapes.

Shape Principles in Spreads

1. Choose a spread you know, or find one online or in a tarot book.

2. Try to identify the four design principles at work in your spread. Look for symmetry, spacing, repetition, and card orientation. What impact do these principles have on the spread? How do they contribute to its effectiveness?

3. Look for geometric patterns within your spread. What role do they play? Is the spread itself a familiar shape?

4. Lay out the pattern of your spread with your tarot cards face down. Experiment with the shape by repositioning some of the cards. See what happens when you break up the existing pattern. You can add and subtract cards as well.

Grid Play

1. Assign a meaning to each row of a three-by-three grid. These meanings should be of the same type or related in some way. Write down your three meanings so you don't forget them.

2. Assign a meaning to each column. These meanings should also go together. Write them down as well.

3. Lay out nine cards in a three-by-three grid. Interpret each card individually according to its assigned row and column meaning. Now interpret the cards in line groups by row and column. See what patterns you notice in this way. How do these group interpretations impact the individual card meanings?

4. Assign three new meanings to the rows and reinterpret. Notice how these changes alter the sense of each card.

5. Assign three new meanings to the columns and again reinterpret. Continue on in this way, or deal out nine new cards and start over.

LESSON 4
SUBJECTS

A tarot reading is an event designed to shed light on a certain subject or subjects. For our purposes, a subject is anything of interest you can name. Some examples are yourself, your health, a project, a friend, a political issue, or a date in time. A subject can be general or specific, past or future, personal or impersonal.

Before doing a reading, it helps to choose a main subject to explore and give it a name. This label then acts as your focus and guide throughout the reading. The name serves as a working title describing the reading in an easy-to-remember format.[5]

Types of Subjects

Tarot subjects can be divided into six main categories: self, others, groups, areas of life, situations, and time periods. The overall meaning of a reading is greatly influenced by the type of its main subject.

Self:

All readings you do *interest* you, but they're not necessarily *about* you.[6] In the self reading, all the cards refer to you personally. They may allude to aspects of your life and environment, but the focus is always on you.

Others:

An "other" reading is about something or someone else, but its message is for you.[7] Usually, the subject is a person, but it can also be an animal, plant, object, or idea. The cards you draw show aspects of the other subject that are important for you to know. They don't show an impersonal picture, but one relevant to you.

---

5 In lesson 7 of *Learning the Tarot*, I describe how to write a question for a reading. A question works in much the same way as a subject name.
6 Throughout this text, "you" means the person a reading is for. When you're doing your own readings, this is naturally you. When you're reading for someone else, "you" or "self" means that person.
7 Lesson 12 covers readings you specifically do for the sake of others.

Groups:

A group reading concerns a group of people with a common identity—for example, a team, work unit, organization, or country. The group may or may not include you. The cards in a group reading refer to the group as a whole.

Areas of Life:

Any area of life can be the subject of a tarot reading. An area of life is a consistent category of experience that endures over time and involves situations that come and go. Some examples are family, career, finances, romance, and health. Areas of life aren't really separate, but sometimes it's useful to look at them this way in a reading.

Situations:

A situation is a unique set of circumstances that exists for a limited period of time—for example, a job opportunity or ceremony. Unlike areas of life, situations don't endure. They come and go as people and events flow through your life. A disagreement with a neighbor is a "situation" in this sense. Four common types are:

> **Problems**—challenges or concerns you perceive as troubling
> **Choices**—decisions, either yes/no or among alternatives
> **Tasks**—projects or endeavors with a certain goal
> **Events**—specific happenings with a clear beginning and end

Situations are the grist of life's mill—the concerns that absorb us day to day. Some, like weddings, are personal. Others, like political elections, are more impersonal. Readings that address a situation can be especially insightful.

Time Periods:

Some time period subjects have a clear beginning and end—for example, days, weeks, months, seasons, and years. Other time periods are more general, such as the past or the future. In the tarot, cards about the future always show probabilities, not givens.

Open Readings

Open readings are not about a specific subject. They're designed to give your inner guide free rein to address any aspect of your experience. But, in a way, these readings do cover a very broad subject—your life as a whole!

Subject Practice

Knowing how to zero in on a main subject for a reading and name it quickly is a useful skill.

1. Look for subjects within your own life, but also within the lives of others.

2. For each subject, identify its type and give it a name or label. People already have names, but you can also label a person by a relationship (Anne's Mom) or function (Director of Engineering).

3. Concentrate on area of life and situation subjects in particular. Try to become clear on the differences between these two.

Subject Lists

Create a list of potential subjects for readings in each of these categories: other people, groups, areas of life, and situations. See Appendix B for sample areas of life. For situations, consider the problems, choices, tasks, and events you are involved in at present. You'll find this list helpful when you go to do a reading, and we'll also be using it in a future exercise.

Other People Practice

1. Shuffle and cut your tarot deck.

2. Hold your cards in one hand, and think about someone you know.

3. Turn over the top card and interpret it as showing "what I most need to be aware of about this person at this time." See the card as telling you something you need to

understand about that person. How is this different from seeing the card as simply about the other person?

4. Continue turning over additional cards for other people, or try focusing on one person for a period of time—perhaps one card a day for a week.

5. Allow the messages in these cards to deepen your relationships.

LESSON 5
THE FLEX SPREAD

Good tarot readers know and use many spreads. Before a reading, they always pause to consider their vast collection, then, without hesitation, zero in on the ideal choice for the occasion—one they know well through years of experience.

A nice theory, but not so true in practice! If you're like me, you probably use the same few spreads over and over. I try new ones from time to time, but somehow they never seem to stick. I always return to my set of "old reliables"— the few spreads I know and trust. They work because they're comfortable and familiar. As I was working on this book, I decided there had to be a better way —some approach to make new spreads easier to learn and use. The result is the flex spread.

The flex spread is a framework for creating layouts. It's similar to a regular spread, but, instead of having fixed positions, it has areas that "hold" positions of different kinds. Figure 6 on the next page shows the six areas of a sample flex-spread layout. The main subject area has one card in the center. It's surrounded by ten quality cards in the quality area. The four areas on each side hold cards for different related subjects of interest. In the next few lessons, I'll talk about each of these areas in detail.

Once you learn the basic structure of the flex spread, you can customize it to fit any reading situation. All you have to do is choose the particular positions you want to go in each area. The result is a "new" layout as simple or elaborate as you wish.

The Main Subject Area

A mandala is a geometric picture or design that symbolizes the cosmos. Most mandalas are circular, suggesting wholeness and unity. A circle also has a center around which everything turns.

The flex spread is mandala-like in that it too has a center called the main subject area. Every flex-spread reading is oriented around at least one main subject. Before

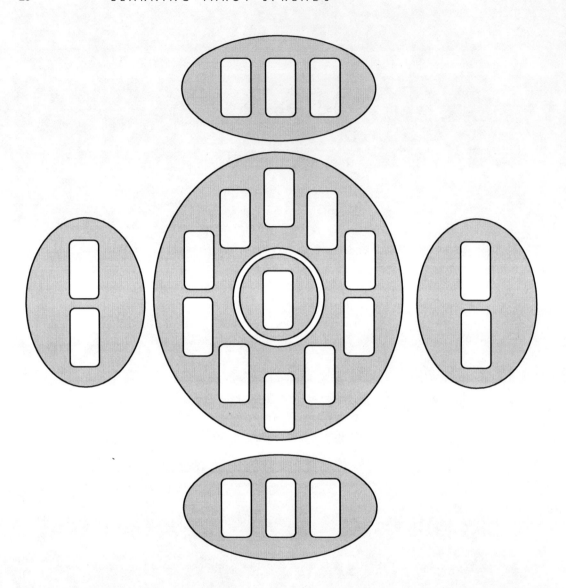

Figure 6. A sample layout showing the six areas of the flex-spread.

you begin a reading, you choose and name this subject and identify its type—person, group, area of life, situation, or time period. You then represent your subject with one position in the center of the spread—the main subject position. This position is only used in this area and is the only kind of position used here.

The main subject position shows a central or key feature of your subject. It symbolizes its essence at the time of the reading. A subject's essence is its heart, so this position goes in the heart of the spread.

The main subject is the only required position in the flex spread. The other areas are optional. In fact, the most basic flex layout consists of just this one card. What could be simpler? One card gives you a quick look at the key feature of a subject. You can focus on any subject type, such as your health (area of life) or a problem (situation). In *Learning the Tarot*, I talk about the daily reading which uses one card as a theme for the day. This is an example of a one-card flex reading about a time period subject.

Multi-Subject Readings

It's possible to explore more than one main subject at the same time using the flex spread. In this case, each subject has its own main subject position. The simplest form has just this one position for every subject. Here are some ideas for multi-subject readings:

Groups:

You can assign one position to every member of a group. A family reading may have one card for each member. A reading about a company may have one for each employee or department. The group identity holds the reading together.

Areas of Life:

A reading about several areas of life is a tarot staple. In the flex spread, you assign one position to each area for an overview of different aspects of your life. When you examine them together, you can notice patterns and trends. See Appendix B for area of life suggestions.

Choices:

A multi-subject reading is ideal when you're facing a decision. You include one main subject position for each option. A yes/no reading would have two cards, one for each case. A decision with four choices would have four cards.

Tasks and events:

You can break up a task or event into units or milestones. Do a three-subject reading about a project with three deadlines. Cover a team's season with a position for each match.

Time periods:

You can divide time periods into units such as months of the year or phases of the moon. See Appendix B for other time period suggestions.

A multi-subject reading is appropriate when you're interested in more than one main subject of the same type. It lets you explore all of them at once. You can create many different flex layouts using just the main subject position, but such readings do lack detail. In the next lesson, we'll look at how you can go deeper using the flex spread.

Main Subject Position Practice

1. Read through the entry for the main subject position in the Position Reference (see page 76). Get to know this position well. Become used to thinking of it as symbolizing the main subject of a reading.

2. Now, look closely at the table for this position. The statements in the middle suggest ways to interpret a main subject card for each subject type. For this exercise, start with line one for self.

3. Shuffle your tarot deck, and hold it face down in your hand.

4. Turn over the top card. As you place it, repeat the statement "'x' is central or key for me right now" but substitute for "x" whatever meaning comes to mind in relation to your card. An example is given for the Four of Pentacles. (For a summary of card meanings, see Appendix C.)

5. Turn over the next card and repeat the statement with a different meaning for that new card.

6. Continue through the deck as long as you like. Note if any statement gives you a quiver of recognition. Perhaps this one has hit home!

7. Now, pick a new subject to work with. Use the statement in the line that matches your subject type. For your career (area of life), you would say "'x' is central or key within my career right now."

Multi-Subject Layout

Design a multi-subject layout using the guidelines in lesson 5.

I. Choose one of the following subject types: group (a group of people with a common bond), area of life (a set of areas of your life), choice (options for a decision you need to make), or task (steps or milestones for a task).

2. Decide on the number of subjects for your reading. A group with four members would have four subjects. A task with seven steps would have seven subjects.

3. Assign a main subject position to each subject. Arrange these positions in any shape that works. (See the Spread Shapes section on page 153 for ideas). If you like, when you're done, use the layout to do an actual reading.

Two Different Weekly Readings

For one week, do two types of weekly readings. On Saturday morning, first do a seven-card multi-subject reading for the whole week. Shuffle, cut, and lay out your cards in a line as in figure 7. Each card represents one day with Saturday on the left through Friday on the right. Write down your choices.

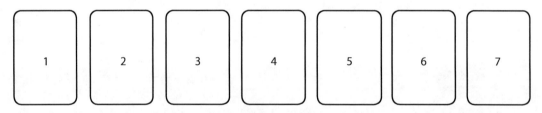

Figure 7. A weekly flex-spread layout.

Next, gather up your cards, reshuffle, cut, and lay out just one card for Saturday. Do a similar single subject reading every morning through Friday.

When the week is over, compare all the cards. How are they similar and different? Which approach was more accurate? More useful? Did you get any repeating cards? The multi-subject reading helps you anticipate the week to come. The daily one-subject readings keep you current as the week progresses. Both methods cover the same time period, but in different ways.

LESSON 6
QUALITIES

The tarot cards are symbols of different kinds of energies. The Emperor suggests a strong, powerful energy with wide influence. The Four of Wands represents a lively, joyous energy of celebration. Each card has its own characteristic "style."

When you do a reading, you identify the energies involved through the cards you draw. The cards picture those energies for you, but not their status at that moment. Are they active or inactive? Growing or fading? Temporary or permanent? Quality positions give you this extra information.

Quality Positions

There are twenty-four quality positions that describe different energetic states. Most are defined in opposing pairs such as beginning and ending, or known and unknown. Quality positions are always assigned to a particular main subject and take their meaning from that subject. For a reading about you, the inside position shows your inner thoughts and emotions. For a self reading about an event, the inside position shows the event's internal dynamics—what's going on behind the scenes.

In the flex spread, quality positions are placed in a circle around the main subject they reference. Pairs are placed opposite each other on either side. The environment and potential quality positions are not paired, but they have permanent locations opposite each other: environment above and potential below the main subject card.

Flex layouts with up to ten qualities are shown starting on page 147. Before a reading, you would decide which quality positions you want to include for your chosen main subject. As you practice with different combinations, you'll discover favorites that work well for you in a variety of circumstances.

A Sample Reading

Let's say you're concerned about your sixteen-year-old daughter. She's been stopped for speeding three times, and you're worried about her driving. You decide to do a reading with this challenging situation as your main subject. You look over the quality choices in the Position Reference (pages 74–75) and decide on two quality pairs that seem useful: contributing to/heading toward, and stabilizing/disrupting. The first pair may help you learn what contributed to this problem and where it's heading; the second may point out what's stable and what's disruptive in the situation.

You draw the Eight of Swords as your main subject card. It pictures the essence of this situation—the overall mood of confusion and powerlessness. You're feeling it, and your daughter probably is too. She's pushing the boundaries of her restrictions.

Stabilizing   Disrupting

Main Subject

Figure 8. Sample flex spread
with two quality pairs.

Contributing To

Heading Toward

Now you add four more cards around the main subject. These are the quality pairs (see figure 8 on facing page). In the Queen of Cups, you see yourself. You believe your love is stabilizing in this situation. In the Fool, you see your daughter. Her apparent folly and "spontaneity" have been disrupting. The Three of Wands shows how her need to explore her limits has contributed to the situation. But, you're heading in a good direction—a new beginning built on trust and practicality (Ace of Pentacles).

Multi-subject Readings

In a multi-subject reading, the qualities for each main subject go in the area immediately around it. Each subject is the center of its own quality "circle." The most useful multi-subject readings duplicate the same positions for each main subject so you can compare the two. Figure 9 shows a layout for two main subjects (cards #1 and #4) with two qualities each. Notice how the positions are grouped so the connections are clear.

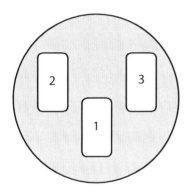
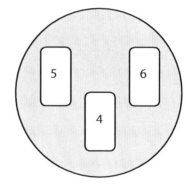

Figure 9. Sample flex spread for two main subjects with two qualities each.

Let's say the main subjects in this case are you and your roommate, and the qualities, avoiding/embracing. The three cards on the left are about you. The center is the main subject, and the cards to either side show what you're avoiding and embracing. The set of cards on the right show the same for your roommate. It's interesting to compare!

Quality positions shed light on a main subject so you can understand its energy dynamics. In the next lesson, we'll talk about ways to explore subjects related to the main one.

EXERCISES:

LESSON 6

Quality Practice During the Day

Try picking a quality to focus on each day. Read its description in the reference section, and then notice that quality as it expresses itself in you, other people, events, and situations. Become aware of it in different contexts.

Another possibility is to think of a tarot card that captures the quality of a moment for you. If someone leaves a meeting in a huff, you may think "disrupting" and see the Seven of Swords (lone-wolf style). Or, you may think "active" and see the Two of Wands (bold). Or perhaps "heading toward" and the Eight of Wands (conclusion). It can be interesting to see what card pops into your head!

Quality Position Practice

This exercise is similar to the main subject practice exercise on page 31.

1. Choose one quality to work with. Read through its keywords and description in the Reference. Now, look at the table for your position.

2. Shuffle your tarot deck, and hold it face down in your hand.

3. Turn over the top card. As you place it, repeat the statement from the middle of the first line of the table (self), but substitute for "x" whatever meaning comes to mind for your card. If you draw the Star and your quality is weak, you might say "Hope is weak within me."

4. Turn over the next card and repeat the statement with a different meaning for that card.

5. Continue through the deck as long as you like. You can also pick a new subject type to work with. Use the statement in the line from the table that matches your chosen type.

Feeling Qualities

I. Go to the summary table for qualities on pages 74–75. This table has brief interpretative statements for all the quality positions.

2. Shuffle your tarot deck, and hold it face down in your hand.

3. Turn over the top card. As you place it, repeat the statement for the first quality (active) using yourself as the main subject type. Substitute for "x" whatever meaning comes to mind for your card. For the Six of Cups, you might say "Innocence is active within me."

4. As you say this statement, feel its meaning within yourself. Create a visceral sense of active innocence, not an intellectual idea of it. Try to make a brief, inner connection.

5. Turn over another card and repeat the statement for the next quality (avoiding) using a meaning for your new card. For the Queen of Pentacles, you might say "I am avoiding nurturing."

6. Continue through the deck as long as you like. You can also pick a new main subject type such as another person or situation.

Quality Layout Study

Examine the quality layouts on pages 147–48 one by one. Notice how the positions adjust with each new quality pair. Look at the order of placement in each case. You may find it helpful to reconstruct each layout using your tarot deck.

Quality Layout Practice

For this exercise, choose a main subject for an imaginary reading and one quality pair you feel will offer insight about that subject.

I. Shuffle and cut your deck.

2. Lay out three cards according to the layout for two qualities on page 147–48.

3. Interpret this layout using your knowledge of the three positions.

Repeat this exercise whenever you have a chance, varying the main subjects and qualities. Gradually, you'll begin learning which positions work best with different subjects. When the time feels right, do an actual reading for yourself using a flex-spread layout with quality positions.

LESSON 7
RELATED SUBJECTS

Most of the time, we view life through the lens of our own consciousness. We assume we're seeing the world as it is, but we're really seeing it colored by our beliefs and expectations. Even when we're aware of the problem, it's still hard to be objective. With the flex spread, you can adopt many different perspectives. You can "look out" from the eyes of any main subject to see from its unique point of view.

In lesson five, you learned how to do a multi main-subject reading. In this type of reading, each subject is an independent unit. The cards for each subject reflect its particular viewpoint. For example, in a simple reading with two main subjects, you might draw the Knight of Swords for you and the Four of Cups for your partner. The Knight suggests you're being direct, even blunt right now. The Four suggests your partner is feeling apathetic. The cards show what each of you is experiencing.

Now, let's change the reading a bit to make your partner a *related* subject. In this case, your partner's card no longer stands on its own. It's related to you as the sole main subject, so you interpret it from your point of view. In this reading, the Four of Cups would show you're feeling apathetic about your partner!

A related subject is always connected to a main subject and draws its meaning from that association. There are four types of related subjects. In the flex spread, each has its own area to one side of the main subject: people (bottom), areas of life (left), situations (top), and time periods (right). Figure 10 on the next page shows a sample flex layout for one main subject with eight related subjects of different kinds. The order of placement begins with the related people at the bottom and goes clockwise through all the areas.

Choosing Related Subjects

You pick the related subjects you want to include before a reading starts. For each main subject, you can have any number of related subjects, or none at all. A related

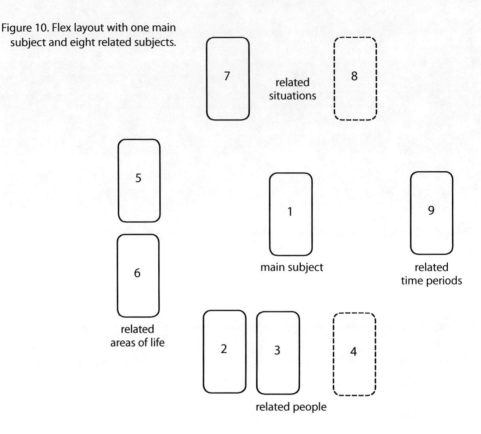

Figure 10. Flex layout with one main subject and eight related subjects.

subject can be named or open. A position is considered to be open unless you name it beforehand. For instance, if you draw the Hanged Man as an open related person, it could show some unspecified person is making a sacrifice in relation to you. You don't know for sure who that person is (though you may be able to guess!). If the position is named (if you assigned someone to it before beginning), you know the sacrifice relates to that particular person.

You can also make yourself a related person in a reading. It's always interesting to see how you're perceived from another subject's point of view!

Potential Related Subjects

A potential related subject is a person or situation that's not yet involved, but may be in the future. A new person may be waiting in the wings to help or hinder. A problem situation may be "sneaking up" on you unexpectedly.

You can find out about such possibilities by designating the right-most related person or situation position as a "potential" before you begin. Cards for these positions are set slightly apart as a reminder of their special status. In figure 10, the dotted positions are potentials (#4 is a person; #8 is a situation). You interpret these cards using the potential subject position (see page 86).

Using Related Subjects

There are countless ways to shed light on a main subject by combining different related subjects.

One main subject/One related subject:

The reading mentioned earlier about you and your partner is an example of this most basic kind of related subject reading. Very simple! (see figure 11). Note that as a related person, your partner's card goes below your card.

```
┌─────────┐
│         │
│    1    │
│         │
└─────────┘


┌─────────┐
│         │
│    2    │
│         │
└─────────┘
```

Figure 11. One main subject/one related person.

One main subject/Two or more related subjects of the same type:

For a situation involving you and two friends, you can make the situation the main subject and each of you a related person (see figure 12 on the next page). For a weekly reading, you can make the entire week your main subject and add seven related time periods—one for each day (see figure 13 on the next page). The related cards show how each day relates to your "theme of the week."

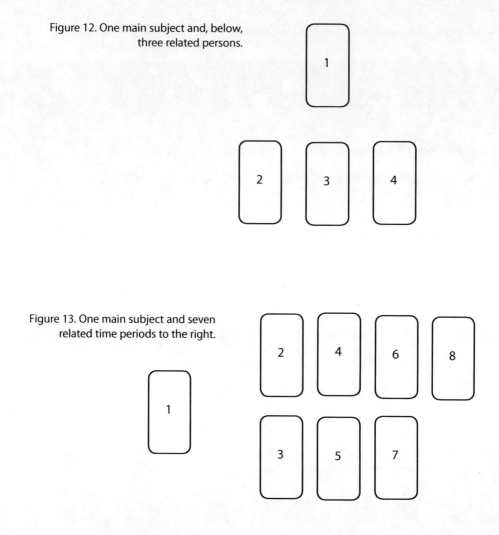

Figure 12. One main subject and, below,
three related persons.

Figure 13. One main subject and seven
related time periods to the right.

One main subject/Two or more related subjects of different types:

You can add a related area of life to your weekly reading to see how this area fits into the week. If you expect to interact with someone during that period, you can also add a named related person card (see figure 14 on the next page).

You can include related subjects in multi-subject readings as well, with each main subject having its own set. Figure 15 shows a revised layout for the reading about you and your roommate from lesson six (see page 35). Note the two new

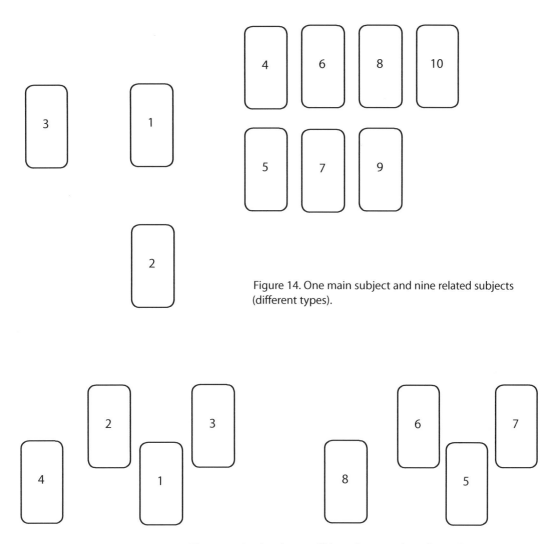

Figure 14. One main subject and nine related subjects (different types).

Figure 15. A related area of life and two qualities for each main subject.

related area-of-life positions (#4 and #8). Each is located near its corresponding main subject (#1 and #5), but outside of the quality positions.

You now have the tools you need to design layouts to explore many connections between the subjects in your life. In the next lesson, we'll see how you can get some guidance on those subjects.

EXERCISES:

LESSON 7

Seeing from Different Points of View

While interacting with someone, imagine for a moment what he or she is experiencing. Do this also for animals, plants, objects, even situations. Think of each as an entity with its own "spirit" and see what that feels like. Become adept at shifting your point of view easily here and there. This ability will serve you well in your readings.

Related Subject Study

Study the related subject position in the Position Reference on page 78. Read the general description and also the sections for each related subject type. Then examine the related subject layouts one by one (pages 143–46). These layouts may look confusing to you at first, but they'll make more sense once you grasp their structure. You may want to recreate each layout using your tarot deck. Next, study the mixed layout on page 146 until you understand each position. Finish with a review of the full flex-spread layout on page 149. It should make sense to you now.

Adding to Your Subject List

Return to the subject list exercise in lesson 4. Update your list if it's old, and add some related subjects to each main subject. Choose from any of the four related-subject types: people, areas of life, situations, and time periods. You can repeat related subjects for different main subjects. You can also include yourself as a related subject. This exercise will leave you with a set of related subjects to use when designing layouts for your readings.

Related Subject Practice

I. Choose a main subject type for an imaginary reading. Shuffle and cut your deck, then lay out two cards as in figure II.

2. Create a simple interpretation for this reading. For example, let's say problem is your type and you draw:

> main-subject type—problem
> main-subject card—Empress
> related-person card—Four of Wands

The Empress suggests a key aspect of this problem is mothering. The Four of Wands shows that some person involved in the problem is feeling free.

Use whatever meanings make sense to you for the cards you draw. You can create a more elaborate interpretation, but it's not necessary.

3. Remove these two cards and lay down two more for a new interpretation. Continue as long as you like. For variety, you can change the main subject or related subject type.

4. When you feel ready, add another related subject. Practice with two subjects of the same type, or two of different types. The goal of this exercise is to become comfortable interpreting related subjects in a variety of settings.

LESSON 8
GUIDANCE

In newspapers, there are two types of articles—news stories and editorials. News stories contain facts; editorials offer opinions. Editors take care to keep the two separate (in theory!). Tarot readings also convey facts and opinions, but, unlike newspapers, they often blend the two. It can be hard to know if a card is telling you "what is" or "what should be."

In the flex spread, facts and opinions are kept separate. Every position you've worked with so far represents a tarot "fact," or factor. A factor position offers a neutral, energetic picture of what is real about some aspect of a main subject. It shows some truth you need to be aware of without bias or adornment.

The guidance position, on the other hand, is an opinion position. It offers counsel, not data. A card in guidance gives you a point of view that comes from the wisdom of your inner guide. Your inner guide knows you intimately and has a grand perspective on your life and purpose. In the guidance position, it communicates something you need to understand about a topic.

Selecting Cards for Guidance

There's no special area for guidance in the flex spread. A guidance card is applied directly to a certain position. You select a position for guidance because you want to understand it better. You need input from your inner guide to help you clarify its meaning. In most readings, certain cards stand out. You know they're important, but you can't quite make them fit with the others. A guidance card can help you understand the message of such a card.

Applying guidance is a separate, optional step. It occurs after you've had a chance to look at all the factors. To choose a position for guidance, you tip the card in that position just a bit. In figure 16 on the next page, three cards have been tipped in this way—#1, #2 and #9. This tipping is your "official" request for guidance. It's a definitive signal to your inner guide.

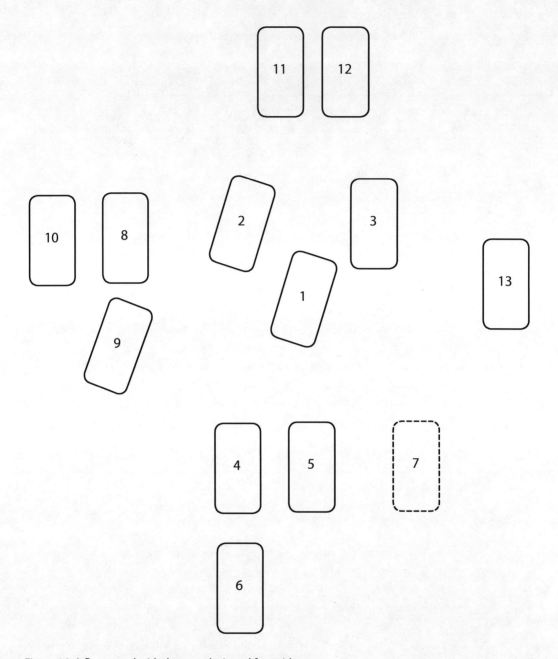

Figure 16. A flex spread with three cards tipped for guidance.

Once you've made your guidance selections, you gather all the unused cards, then reshuffle and recut. It's important to take this extra step because, by tipping cards for guidance, you have changed the course of your reading. When you first shuffled your deck, your request for guidance had not yet been made, so the original card order is out of date. You need to begin again symbolically.

When your deck is ready, lay out your guidance cards *in the same order* as the tipped cards. For the layout in figure 16, you would place guidance for the main subject first (1), then the quality card (2), and finally the related area-of-life card (9).

Place each guidance card over the lower right corner of its associated factor card to emphasize the connection. Once you've placed all the guidance, you can move the cards around while you interpret.

You may think the more guidance, the better, but this isn't really so. You can overwhelm yourself with advice! Too many guidance cards diminish the value of each one. A good rule of thumb is to have no more than one guidance card for every six or seven positions.

Guidance applied to the main subject position has special significance. This position symbolizes a main subject directly and serves as the focal point for a reading. So, its guidance carries extra weight. It extends out to "cover" all the other cards.

Sample Reading with Guidance

You've done a small reading about your finances to better understand this area of your life right now. You chose for your layout one main subject (your finances), two qualities (blocking and clearing), and one named related person (you).

The cards you've drawn are shown in figure 17 on the next page. Most of this reading makes sense to you. You've been persevering in trying to improve your finances (Nine of Wands), but it still feels like an uphill fight. You've been moderate in your spending (Temperance) and juggling all your bills to clear your debt (Two of Pentacles).

The only card you don't understand is the Ten of Pentacles. How can wealth be blocking? You decide to ask for guidance about this card and draw the Seven of Cups. Now you see it's wishful thinking about affluence that is blocking you. The desire to be free of money problems is making you edgy.

To interpret a guidance card, you must tap directly into your intuition. A guidance card can show a new approach, offer a note of caution, or simply encourage. Only you can assess the guidance in each case.

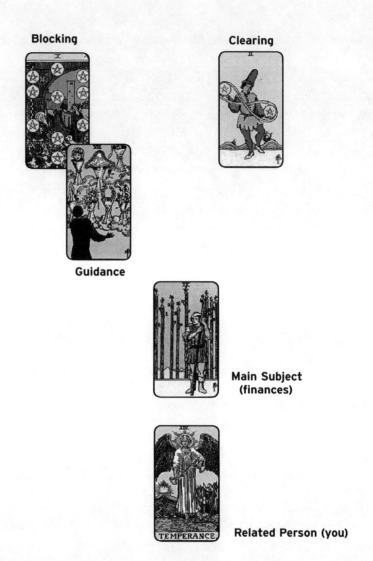

Blocking

Clearing

Guidance

Main Subject (finances)

Related Person (you)

Figure 17. Sample flex layout with guidance.

You can assume guidance comes with your best interests at heart. It doesn't tell you what to do or think. It's offered with loving wisdom as something for you to ponder. You're always free to respond in whatever way you think best, without judgment from your inner guide.

Guidance and Factors in Spreads

Choose a spread you know, or find one online or in a tarot book. Try to identify which positions are factors and which are guidance. See if a clear distinction is made between the two in the author's definitions. Think about your own readings in light of this difference. Do you tend to blend factors and guidance? Does this matter to you?

Guidance Study

Study the guidance position in the Position Reference on page 91. Read the general description and look through the tables to see how guidance works with the different position types.

Factor vs. Guidance

The goal of this exercise is to help you become clear on the difference between a factor and guidance when interpreting a card. Vary the exercise by focusing on a subject type other than yourself.

1. Shuffle and cut your tarot deck. Hold your cards in one hand, and turn over the top card.

2. First, interpret this card as a factor. Say: "_____ is an actual part of my life right now because _____." Fill in the first blank with some meaning you see in the card. Fill in the second blank with a brief comment about how this statement is true for you right now.

    For the Eight of Pentacles, you might say "Details are an actual part of my life right now because my reports at work have to be exactly right."

3. Interpret the card again, but this time as guidance. Say: "The idea of _____ is helpful to me right now because _____." Fill in the first blank with the same

card meaning you used before, but this time fill in the second blank with some guiding principle.

For the Eight of Pentacles, you might say "The idea of details is helpful to me right now because it reminds me to pay attention to small matters even if they seem insignificant."

Guidance Practice

1. Choose a main subject for an imaginary reading and identify its type. Shuffle and cut your cards and place the top card in front of you as your main subject.

2. Tip this card to request guidance, and turn over a guidance card.

3. Create a simple interpretation for this "reading." For instance, in a reading of the other person type, you draw the Queen of Cups as the main subject and the Ace of Pentacles as guidance. The Ace implies that this loving and tenderhearted person (Queen of Cups) may need to be more practical and start focusing on everyday matters.

4. Use whatever meanings make sense to you for the cards you draw. When you're done, remove the two cards, and lay down two more for a new reading. You can vary this exercise by changing your main subject type.

More Guidance Practice

This exercise is similar to the previous exercise, but focuses on positions other than the main subject.

1. Prepare your deck as before, then lay out a main subject card and a related person card.

2. Shuffle, cut, and then apply a guidance card to the related person. Create a simple interpretation.

3. When you're done, remove these cards, and lay out two more. Again apply a guidance card to the related person.

4. For variety, switch at some point to a new related subject, such as a time period. When you're comfortable with related subjects, move on to qualities. Return to this exercise whenever you have a chance to help you progress.

LESSON 9
PLANNING A LAYOUT

Now that you know all the areas of the flex spread, it's time to look at how to plan and choose a layout for a reading. Before beginning, take a moment to center yourself and think about the reading to come. The goal is to become clear about your intentions. Here are a few questions to help you focus:

What's the purpose of this reading?
What are my hopes and fears right now?
What subject(s) am I most interested in right now?
How much detail do I want from the cards?
Do I just want information, or do I want guidance too?

Choosing Your Main Subject

You must choose the main subject(s) for your reading. Use the conclusions you reached earlier to guide you. Decide whether to focus on just one main subject or more.

Choose one main subject if *any* of the following are true:

You have only one main area of interest right now.
If you're interested in just one thing, then it's easy—you have your main subject.

You have no special area of interest at the moment.
If you have no special subject you want to explore, choose one general main subject such as "my life" or "the present."

You want to explore one subject in detail.
If you want to include many qualities or related subjects, focus on just one main subject.

Choose multiple main subjects if *all* the following are true:

> You're equally interested in two or more subjects of the same type.
> You want to compare two or more subjects side-by-side.
> You don't need to explore your subjects in great detail.

Once you've identified your main subjects, give each a short label.[8]

Main Subject Type

As you choose your main subject, consider its type as well. Here are some points to keep in mind:

Self:

Choose a self reading if you're mainly interested in your inner experience and the aspects of your own life.

Other person:

Focus on someone else if you're concerned or curious about that person. Remember, you'll receive the information and guidance you need to consider that person.

Group:

A group reading is best if you want to understand from the perspective of a group as a whole.

Area of life:

Choose an area of life if it's of special interest to you in a general way, not because of a particular person or situation within that area.

Time period:

A time-period reading is best if you're interested in all the issues and events of a certain expanse of time.

---

8 You can also write a question about your subject as an extra point of focus. See lesson 7 in *Learning the Tarot*.

Situation:

Focus on a situation if you have a choice to make, or you're involved in a specific matter. It will help you understand what to do and how to respond.

Choosing or Designing a Layout

You can always use a previously designed layout. You'll find some examples in the Sample Flex-Spread Layouts section on page 143. You can also create or modify a layout. Consider the following:

Main subjects:

You need one main subject position for every main subject. Arrange multiple main subjects in a shape that works for your number of positions.

Qualities (optional):

Decide which quality pairs, if any, you want for each main subject. Also consider using the environment or potential quality positions.

Related subjects (optional):

Decide how many related subjects, if any, to include in each of the four areas—people, areas of life, time periods, and situations. Choose those you want to be named. The rest will be open. Consider including a related person position for yourself. Also decide if you need a potential person or a potential situation.

Play with different layout possibilities. You'll know you've found a good combination when the layout feels comfortable and right. When you're satisfied, make a permanent record of your layout. For every position, note the type, location, name (if any), and placement order. You can use the layout planning form in Appendix E.

Learning Your Layout

Try to memorize your layout before using it. Visualize the positions and see yourself placing cards in order. You can practice using a playing card deck or with your tarot cards face down. (You don't want to create a reading by using them face up.)

Clarity is so important in the tarot. I can't emphasize this too much! Your reading will flow better if you know your layout well. This familiarity allows you to pay attention to your intuition rather than procedural details. But, don't be concerned if you do need to refer to your notes during a reading.

At first, choosing and learning a layout takes a little time, but the process gets easier. Soon, the best layout for an occasion will occur to you naturally, perhaps even while you're simply thinking about your reading. Also, over time, you will gradually put together a set of favorite layouts that you know work for you.

Single or Multiple Main Subjects?

For each of the following circumstances, decide whether you would choose a single or multiple main subject reading. Then name the main subject(s) and their type. See Appendix A (page 161) for my suggestions.

    Example:

      I wonder how March and April are shaping up for me?

      Multiple—March and April (time periods)

1. I don't have a special interest right now. I just want to know what's going on for me.
2. I want to find out everything I can about my upcoming concert.
3. I can't decide whether to say yes or no to Arnold.
4. I'm tired all the time. I wonder if there's something wrong?
5. I need a quick look at the difference between the three teams.
6. I don't need a lot of detail, but I'd like some insight into each of my two grandchildren.
7. All I can think about is this problem with my dog.
8. I want to explore my past.
9. Why do I feel so depressed?
10. The meeting is in 10 minutes. I need something on each of my four projects.

Layout Design Practice

Design a layout for each of the ten scenarios in Table 1 on page 58. Arrange the positions according to the flex-spread structure. See pages 162–64 for my suggestions.

Plan a Reading

Design a flex-spread layout for yourself using the guidelines in lesson 9. Use the layout planning form in Appendix E. When you feel ready, try your layout in a reading following the procedure in Appendix D.

Table 1. Practice Layout Elements

Scenario	Main Subject(s)	Qualities	Related Subjects
1	self	----	my diet
2	my finances	enduring temporary potential quality	----
3	moving to Chicago moving to DC moving to Boston	(for each choice) new old	----
4	book project	avoiding embracing	potential situation
5	January	active inactive	----
6	work assignment	environment stabilizing disrupting blocking clearing	week one week two week three
7	my nephew	----	his older sister his younger sister his mom me
8	fight with John	contributing to moving toward	me John our relationship last month's fight
9	my four classes	----	----
10	self	weak strong	my partner my health

LESSON 10
SERIAL READINGS

Serial readings offer you a way to explore a group of subjects in great depth. The premise is simple. After completing a reading, you decide if you'd like to continue the session. If so, you choose any subject card from those already drawn and make that card the main subject of a new reading.

There are two kinds of serial readings. In the first, you choose a single main subject card to focus on from among those in a multi-subject layout. For example, let's say you've done a three-card reading to look at three areas of your life—work, romance, and health. You've drawn the Tower as the romance card. You wonder what this is all about. You decide to find out by doing a serial reading focused on just the Tower.

In the second type of serial reading, you choose a related subject card to focus on. For example, in a reading for yourself, you've drawn the totally unexpected Lovers card for a related situation. You think this card may be suggesting you're seeing this situation in a sexual light. You're curious about that, so you make the Lovers the main subject of a new reading. Now you can examine this situation in more detail.

To do a serial reading, simply choose one subject card on which to focus—main or related—and set that card aside. This card should not already have any quality or related subject cards associated with it, but keep any guidance card.

Next, gather up all the rest of the cards. When you're done, put the retained card with its guidance, if any, back in front of you as the main subject for your new reading. Then, continue as if starting from the beginning. The only difference now is that your main subject card (and its guidance) is already chosen for you. It's important to reshuffle and cut between readings. Don't keep the old arrangement of cards.

A serial reading is always based on a subject card from a prior reading. Quality cards are not suitable. You should keep the name and type of the card you pick as well. A time period stays a time period of the same duration. A related person card for Jeff becomes the center of a reading about Jeff. A potential situation card stays a potential situation.

A serial reading can take any form you like. You can use the same layout as the first reading, or change it. You can make the serial reading smaller or larger than the first. The only requirement is that you hold over at least one card as your main subject. You can carry over more than one for a multi-subject serial reading, but they should all be of the same subject type.

You can do serial readings as long as you have the time and inclination. You can explore different subjects from your original reading, one after the other. Or, you can take a subject from a serial reading and continue on from there. Either way, you create a series of readings that are interconnected through their subjects.

A reading is an energetic event that reflects a certain moment in time. Ideally, that "moment" should be one unbroken experience. Try to complete all your serial readings in one sitting, if at all possible. Be sure to write down each reading before you move on to the next so you can look for patterns and connections later. The same cards often repeat in revealing ways.

It can be tempting to do a lot of serial readings. It's fascinating to watch the cards unfold in various guises, but do commit to devoting time to every reading you do. You honor the tarot process in this way. Serial readings give you a chance to go deeper into the subjects that concern you and let you look at all their relationships from different perspectives.

Serial Reading Choices

For each of the ten layouts for scenarios 1–10 starting on page 162, decide which positions in each are valid choices to become the main subject of a serial reading. My suggestions are on page 165.

Serial Reading Practice

When you have some free time, select one of the layouts for scenarios 1–10 starting on page 162. Do a "reading" based on your selection following the procedure in Appendix D.

When you reach step 13, choose a card for a serial reading and follow the guidelines in lesson 10. Continue doing serial readings as long as you like. Choose other cards from your first reading (if any), or from those that follow. Be sure to write down your cards from each reading.

Doing Your Own Serial Reading

Look for a chance to do a serial reading after one of your own readings. Don't force one artificially, but do give the process a try if the opportunity arises. Later, take time to study the readings and all the cards. Look for patterns and connections. A serial reading can offer a new dimension of insight in your tarot work.

LESSON 11
VARIATIONS

Here are some reading variations to try after you're comfortable with the basic flex-spread procedure.

As-You-Go Readings

As-you-go readings emphasize intuition. Instead of planning a reading ahead of time, you make all your decisions on the fly. Just select and name a main subject. From then on, the reading is spontaneous.

After placing your main subject card, pause for a moment to let your intuition reveal your next move. Wait for an inner impulse to tell you where the next card should go. It may feel like a related person card for your friend Alex, If so, put the card in the related person area and say aloud: "This is Alex." If it feels like a blocking quality, put the card in the qualities area and say: "This is what's blocking right now." You can put all cards in one area, or skip around. Keep going until you sense it's time to stop. If you like, you can add some structure to the process by going systematically, area by area, through the spread. Allow time for cards within each area to reveal themselves before moving on to the next.

As-you-go readings require faith. You have to trust your impulses and let the reading unfold as it will. It does get easier with practice and can leave you with a heightened sense of connection with your inner guide.

Double-Deck Readings

Double-deck readings use two decks instead of one. Any two decks will work, even non-tarot decks, as long as both decks are different. You don't want to risk mixing the cards. Some decks, such as the Rider Waite and Universal Waite, have versions in different sizes. For these, you can use one large and one small deck.

Before beginning, assign each area of your layout to one or the other of the two decks—for instance, one deck for factors and one for guidance, or one deck for subjects and one for qualities. Shuffle and cut each deck separately. Place all the cards for a given area from the appropriate deck. When done, you'll have a mixture of cards in front of you.

Using two decks can produce some interesting results. The same cards can appear in two places, doubling the energies involved. Moreover, new meanings can arise when you use a deck with unusual cards.

Partner or Group Readings

You can explore a subject with another person or group. Each participant must have his or her own tarot deck. Decide among yourselves what main subject you want to investigate together. Try to agree on related subjects and qualities as well. The goal is for everyone to use the same layout so you can compare insights afterward.

It's a good idea in these readings to examine a common bond or reason for being together. This may be a relationship, task, event, mutual acquaintance, or situation. An alternative is for each person to be the main subject of his or her own reading, with the other people as related subjects.

It helps to have a leader who guides everyone through the process. When the time comes to place the cards, all participants should have their own space and time to work with their cards. Then, when everyone is ready, the sharing can begin.

It's important to be respectful and empathetic when sharing. Don't force anyone to contribute, but try to make the most of this chance to learn about each other. If a seemingly negative card appears, view it as a positive opportunity to air concerns without judgment. Be prepared for some interesting discussions as you explore the results!

LESSON 12
READING FOR OTHERS

Once, years ago, I went to a coworker's office to say goodbye on my last day of work. I happened to mention the tarot, and he immediately whisked me into his room for a reading. It turned out to be a beautiful session—meaningful for both of us. In that half hour, I got to know this man better than during all the time I'd worked with him.

Once you start studying the tarot, sooner or later, someone's going to ask you for a reading. People are curious—about the process and about themselves. You may jump at the opportunity or hesitate, wondering if you can handle this new direction. In this lesson, I'd like to share my thoughts about reading for someone else.

Seekers

In tarot literature, a person asking for a reading is often called the "querent," someone making a query. I prefer the term "seeker." For our purposes, then, a seeker is simply someone who asks you for a reading.

You may encounter two kinds of seekers: those you know (friends, relations, neighbors, or coworkers) and those you don't know (strangers who ask for a reading for whatever reason).[9] Treat both the same, as much as possible.

For seekers you know, you can't help being aware of your "real" relationship. Don't jeopardize that relationship in any way, but do try to set it aside for the moment. Treat the reading as an event out of time for both of you.

Seekers can be eager or hesitant, open or closed, quiet or talkative, laughing or somber. Don't let any of these differences concern you. They're simply expressions of personality. If someone seems nervous, be calm and reassuring.

---

9 A third type is the paying client, but this type is outside the scope of this lesson.

The Seeker's Goal

In readings, we come face to face with the mysterious. People remember readings with great feeling—especially their first. They can often recall details years later. My mother visited a storefront reader in downtown San Francisco when she was just eighteen. She talked about that reading off and on her whole life. It was a whim of the moment, but it was special to her because it opened a door into the unknown.

Seekers may request readings for many reasons, but they only ask when they are ready to look below the surface of their lives—at least a little. Even the most casual seekers are drawn for this purpose, although they may not acknowledge it. Those who are totally uninterested will never cross your path. So readings should always be done at the seeker's request. Never force or even encourage a reading. The desire for insight needs to come from the seeker.

Inner Guides

A tarot reading actually involves four "entities"—you, the seeker, and both your inner guides. It's a group event!

Your inner guide is by your side throughout the reading. It sends you intuitive messages that you pass on to the seeker, who absorbs those understandings with the help of his or her own inner guide. Together, the four of you create an event that is meaningful on many levels.

Choosing a Layout

For most seekers, a good, all-purpose main subject is "my life." Occasionally, someone will be concerned about something in particular and ask you to focus on that topic. This is more common when you read for someone regularly. In this case, pick a main subject and type that suits the seeker's concern.

Choose a layout based on a quick assessment of the moment. Here are some points to consider:

What is the reading environment?

Keep the reading "lighter" when the environment is public or casual. Deeply personal readings are best kept for private moments.

How much time do we have?

Use small layouts if time is an issue so you can finish without feeling rushed. Leave time for the guidance step as well.

What is the seeker's stated goal, if any?

Always accommodate a seeker's spoken requests for the reading, if possible.

What do I know about the seeker?

Bear in mind what you know of the seeker, but don't let preconceived ideas get in the way. Things are not always as they seem!

Do I have any pre-reading "flashes"?

Be aware of intuitive flashes before a reading. These can arrive as you're sitting down, or even days before! Accommodate these in your layout.

How much energy do I have?

Assess your energy level. Don't take on a complicated or heavy reading when you're feeling drained. Also, keep the layout simple if you have many readings to do in a row.

Be prepared with a few all-purpose layouts you know well. You can use one as is or adapt it to suit the moment. A good layout offers a variety of opportunities for open-ended insights in different areas. See pages 151–52 for a few suggestions.

If you have time, you can do a small preliminary reading about a few area-of-life subjects, then follow up with a serial reading about one of them.

The Process

You can follow the same basic process outlined in Appendix D, but delete time-consuming steps such as taking notes and writing a summary statement. These break up the flow.

The seeker should shuffle and cut the cards, if possible. Hand her the cards, and tell her to shuffle until she feels ready to stop. Then, direct her through the cut and have her hand the cards back to you. I recommend having a separate deck devoted to readings you do for others.

You should lay out the cards. I try to sit next to the seeker so we can look at the cards together. This arrangement fosters sharing. If you must sit opposite, try to place the cards so you can both see them easily.

Your Role

Your role as the reader is to help the seeker make discoveries through the cards. You don't have to be a tarot expert to achieve this goal! It's the desire to be of service that counts.

The secret is to keep the focus on the seeker and away from yourself. This is easier said than done. Your pesky ego will get in the way by saying such things as:

"You don't know what you're doing."
"Who do you think you are? You're just a beginner."
"These interpretations are really lame."
"He's not pleased with your efforts."
"Other readers are better than you."
"This is really going well. I'm pretty impressive."
"I'm special because I can do this."

Your ego can come up with many such "helpful" comments. If one crosses your mind, simply smile to yourself, let it go, and return to the seeker. With experience, you'll "forget" yourself more and more, and, ironically, become more confident and relaxed.

Create an environment in which the seeker feels free to contribute. Some won't want to, but others will become engaged and vocal. Let the seeker know what you're doing as appropriate, but it's best not to get too wordy. Be truthful, but positive. Never say that something is absolutely going to happen, as this can't be known. Leave the seeker with a hopeful orientation toward the future.

Turn to your inner guide frequently. It will help you know what to do if you trust and stay open. Have faith in its wise counsel. Know the reading will work out just as it should.

I encourage you to try reading for someone else if an opportunity presents itself. In our rushed society, there are so few occasions to sit with someone and share. Take this one when you can!

Becoming Aware of Your Ego

As you go about your daily affairs, practice becoming aware of your ego's comments. These are thoughts you have about yourself that are critical or self-inflating. When one of these thoughts comes to mind, acknowledge it, and then gently set it aside. Don't engage the thought, just move quietly past it. If you like, you can turn your thoughts instead to your wise and loving inner guide. This practice will serve you well when you read for others.

Sample Layouts

Study the sample layouts for readings for others on pages 151–52. Pick one to work with and practice placing cards in the pattern until you know it well. Visualize doing a reading with it. Add, delete, or adjust positions that don't work for you.

If you're already reading for others, try introducing one of these layouts when the opportunity presents itself. If you haven't read for someone yet, you can have one of these layouts ready to fall back on should the need arise.

Reading for an Imaginary Friend

Practice doing a reading for an imaginary friend. If you like, you can use the layout you selected for the last exercise or try a new one. Go through the entire reading procedure in Appendix D. Think about each step as you go. Adjust or delete any that don't work for you.

Pretend your friend is sitting right next to you. This is most effective if you really get into the role. Feel and act as if the reading were actually happening. Then, when you do read for someone, the process will feel familiar. Of course, a real reading is going to be unpredictable, but you'll be ready!

PART 2

POSITIONS,
LAYOUTS,
AND
SPREAD SHAPES

POSITION REFERENCE

Position Summary Tables

These tables contain short interpretative statements for all the positions. To check a card in a reading, find its position in column one. Column two will suggest a way to interpret the card in that position. "X" stands for whatever meaning you see in the card at that time. Column three gives the page number for each position in the reference.

Table 2. Subject Positions and Guidance

If the position is:	a card in this position suggests, at the time of the reading: ("x" = some meaning of the card)	Page number
Main Subject	"x" is central or key for the main subject	76
Related Person	this related person means "x" to the main subject	78
Related Area of Life	this related area of life means "x" to the main subject	80
Related Situation	this related situation means "x" to the main subject	82
Related Time Period	this related time period means "x" to the main subject	84
Potential Person	this potential person may mean "x" to the main subject at some point	86
Potential Situation	this potential situation may mean "x" to the main subject at some point	88
Guidance	"x" as guidance helps me understand what the target position and its card mean to the main subject	90

Table 3. Quality Positions: A-H

If the position is:	a card in this position suggests, at the time of the reading: ("x" = some meaning of the card)	Page number
Active	"x" is active within the main subject	94
Avoiding	the main subject is avoiding "x"	96
Beginning	"x" is beginning within the main subject	98
Blocking	"x" is blocking within the main subject	100
Clearing	"x" is clearing the way within the main subject	102
Contributing to	"x" has contributed to the current state of the main subject	104
Disrupting	"x" is disrupting within the main subject	106
Embracing	the main subject is embracing "x"	108
Ending	"x" is ending within the main subject	110
Enduring	"x" is enduring within the main subject	112
Environment	the environment surrounding the main subject is "x"	114
Heading toward	the main subject is heading toward "x"	116

Table 3. Quality Positions: I-Z

If the position is:	a card in this position suggests, at the time of the reading: ("x" = some meaning of the card)	Page number
Inactive	"x" is inactive within the main subject	118
Inside	"x" is going on inside the main subject	120
Known	the main subject knows "x" "x" is known about the main subject	122
New	"x" is new within the main subject	124
Old	"x" is old within the main subject	126
Outside	the main subject is "x" on the outside	128
Potential	"x" is a potential within the main subject	130
Stabilizing	"x" is stabilizing within the main subject	132
Strong	"x" is strong within the main subject	134
Temporary	"x" is temporary within the main subject	136
Unknown	the main subject doesn't know "x" "x" is unknown about the main subject	138
Weak	"x" is weak within the main subject	141

SUBJECT POSITIONS

Main Subject

Keywords:

central issue, core, crux, essence, focus, gist, heart of the matter, key, main idea, spirit, substance, theme

Description:

The main subject position has two purposes. First, it symbolizes the main subject of a reading and serves as a visual reminder of that subject within a spread. Second, it shows the central issue or spirit of the main subject at the time of a reading. This position captures the heart of the matter—a subject's key idea or theme. It doesn't show the essence of a subject for all time, just what's central in some important way at the moment.

For instance, the Empress may show an energy of mothering or abundance is central to you as the main subject. The Chariot may show the essence of some problem is self-assertion. Sometimes, a main subject card describes the subject as a whole. At other times, it refers to some person who's playing a key role. The Knight of Wands can show a passionate charmer is central in some area of your life.

Reversed:

A lack of something is the central or key factor for the main subject. The essence of a group may be a lack of friendship (reversed Three of Cups). The spirit of a time period may be a lack of conformity (reversed Hierophant).

Flex-spread usage:

In the center of the flex spread surrounded by its qualities and related subjects, if any.

Table 4. MAIN SUBJECT POSITION by Main Subject Type

If the Main Subject type is:	the Main Subject card suggests: ("x" = some meaning of the card)	Example – Four of Pentacles (sample meaning = control)
Self	"x" is central or key for me right now	control is central or key for me right now
Other Person	"x" is central or key for this person right now, from my point of view	control is central or key for this person right now, from my point of view
Group	"x" is central or key for the group as a whole right now	control is central or key for the group as a whole right now
Area of Life	"x" is central or key within this area of my life right now	control is central or key within this area of my life right now
Time Period	"x" is central or key within this time period	control is central or key within this time period
Problem	"x" is central or key within this problem right now "x" is central or key right now for someone involved in this problem	control is central or key within this problem right now control is central or key right now for someone involved in this problem
Choice	"x" is central or key right now when it comes to this choice "x" is central or key for me right now when it comes to this choice	control is central or key right now when it comes to this choice control is central or key for me right now when it comes to this choice
Project/Task	"x" is central or key within this project right now "x" is central or key right now for someone involved in this project	control is central or key within this project right now control is central or key right now for someone involved in this project
Event	"x" is central or key within this event right now "x" is central or key right now for someone involved in this event	control is central or key within this event right now control is central or key right now for someone involved in this event

RELATED SUBJECT

Keywords:

central issue, core, crux, essence, focus, gist, heart of the matter, key, main idea, spirit, substance, theme

Description:

The related subject position symbolizes a related subject in a reading. It shows a central or key feature of that subject from the point of view of the main subject at that time. A card in this position doesn't describe how the related subject sees itself or how a third party may see it. It shows what the main subject feels, believes, or expects about the related subject.

There are four types of related subjects: people, areas of life, situations, and time periods. All use this same position type. A related subject can be named or open. If named, it stands for a particular subject—one you designate before a reading begins. If open, the position represents any subject of its type.

Related Person

A related person is someone known to or involved with the main subject at the time of the reading. You may view a related person as a wise counselor (King of Cups) or friend (Three of Cups). For a project, someone may represent a responsibility (Justice) or source of worry (Nine of Swords). A support group may see one participant as self-absorbed (Four of Cups) or loving (Page of Cups).

Reversed:

A related person lacking some quality as far as the main subject is concerned. You may see someone as failing to act (reversed Magician). A community group may feel a related person is demonstrating a lack of caution (reversed Knight of Pentacles).

Flex-spread usage:

Below the main subject and its qualities, if any.

Table 5. RELATED PERSON by Main Subject Type

If the Main Subject type is:	a Related Person suggests: ("x" = some meaning of the card)	Example – Ten of Cups (sample meaning = joy)
Self	this person means "x" to me	this person means joy to me
Other Person	this related person means "x" to the main subject person, from my point of view	this related person means joy to the main subject person, from my point of view
Group	this person means "x" to the group as a whole	this person means joy to the group as a whole
Area of Life	this person means "x" to this area of life	this person means joy to this area of life
Time Period	this person tends to mean "x" during this time period	this person tends to mean joy during this time period
Problem	this person means "x" within this problem this person means "x" to someone involved in this problem	this person means joy within this problem this person means joy to someone involved in this problem
Choice	this person means "x" when it comes to this choice this person means "x" to me when it comes to this choice	this person means joy when it comes to this choice this person means joy to me when it comes to this choice
Project/Task	this person means "x" within this project this person means "x" to someone involved in this projectt	this person means joy within this project this person means joy to someone involved in this project
Event	this person means "x" within this event this person means "x" to someone involved in this event	this person means joy within this event this person means joy to someone involved in this event

Related Area of Life

A related area of life is an area connected to the main subject in some way at the time of the reading. Areas of life are usually named. Your career may be a creative area of life for you (Page of Wands). In a reading for your son, his health may feel like a rebirth to him during recovery (Judgment). Someone involved in a task may need deeper meaning in the area of his spiritual life (Eight of Cups).

Reversed:

A related area of life lacking some quality as far as the main subject is concerned. You may be feeling a lack of attraction in a relationship (reversed Two of Cups). Someone may be failing to prepare quietly for a rainy day in the area of finances (reversed Four of Swords).

Flex-spread usage:

To the left of the main subject and its qualities, if any.

Table 6. RELATED AREA OF LIFE by Main Subject Type

If the Main Subject type is:	a Related Area of Life suggests: ("x" = some meaning of the card)	Example – Five of Swords (sample meaning = open dishonor)
Self	this area of life means "x" to me	this area of life is dishonorable to me
Other Person	this area of life means "x" to this other person, from my point of view	this area of life is dishonorable to this other person, from my point of view
Group	this area of life means "x" to the group as a whole	this area of life is dishonorable to the group as a whole
Area of Life	this related area of life means "x" to this area of life	this related area of life is dishonorable within the main area of life
Time Period	this area of life tends to mean "x" during this time period	this area of life tends to be dishonorable during this time period
Problem	this area of life means "x" within this problem

this area of life means "x" to someone involved in this problem | this area of life is dishonorable within this problem

this area of life is dishonorable to someone involved in this problem |
| Choice | this area of life means "x" when it comes to this choice

this area of life means "x" to me when it comes to this choice | this area of life is dishonorable when it comes to this choice

this area of life is dishonorable to me when it comes to this choice |
| Project/Task | this area of life means "x" within this project

this area of life means "x" to someone involved in this project | this area of life is dishonorable within this project

this area of life is dishonorable to someone involved in this project |
| Event | this area of life means "x" within this event

this area of life means "x" to someone involved in this event | this area of life is dishonorable within this event

this area of life is dishonorable to someone involved in this event |

Related Situation

A related situation is some situation of interest to the main subject at the time of a reading. It can be a problem, choice, project, or event. A card in this position can refer to the situation itself or to someone involved in it.

A related problem may be a test of your personal beliefs (Lovers). A related event may involve someone who is showing competence (Three of Pentacles). In a reading for your husband, a related career choice may represent greater control to him (Four of Pentacles).

Reversed:

A related situation lacking some quality as far as the main subject is concerned. Calm diplomacy may be missing in some related problem (reversed King of Cups). Someone involved in a task-related situation may lack balance (reversed Temperance).

Flex-spread usage:

Above the main subject and its qualities, if any.

Table 7. RELATED SITUATION by Main Subject Type

If the Main Subject type is:	a Related Situation suggests: ("x" = some meaning of the card)	Example –Three of Pentacles (sample meaning = teamwork)
Self	this situation means "x" to me	this situation means teamwork to me
Other Person	this situation means "x" to this other person, from my point of view	this situation means teamwork to this other person, from my point of view
Group	this situation means "x" to the group as a whole	this situation means teamwork to the group as a whole
Area of Life	this situation means "x" within this area of life	this situation means teamwork within this area of life
Time Period	this situation tends to mean "x" during this time period	this situation tends to mean teamwork during this time period
Problem	this situation means "x" within this problem	this situation means teamwork within this problem
	this situation means "x" to someone involved in this problem	this situation means teamwork to someone involved in this problem
Choice	this situation means "x" when it comes to this choice	this situation means teamwork when it comes to this choice
	this situation means "x" to me when it comes to this choice	this situation means teamwork to me when it comes to this choice
Project/Task	this situation means "x" within this project	this situation means teamwork within this project
	this situation means "x" to someone involved in this project	this situation means teamwork to someone involved in this project
Event	this situation means "x" within this event	this situation means teamwork within this event
	this situation means "x" to someone involved in this event	this situation means teamwork to someone involved in this event

Related Time Period

A related time period is a stretch of time of interest to the main subject. The period can be in the past, present, or future, but its meaning is what's true at the time of the reading. In the future time period, the Six of Pentacles may suggest having resources as a future issue. The Page of Wands in "May 3, 2003" suggests that date may represent courage to you at the time of the reading.

Reversed:

The related time period represents a lack of something during that time. Vacation week may mean a lack of hassles to you (reversed Five of Wands). The day of a big test may represent a period of little spontaneity (reversed Fool).

Flex-spread usage:

To the right of the main subject and its qualities, if any.

Table 8. RELATED TIME PERIOD by Main Subject Type

If the Main Subject type is:	a Related Time Period suggests: ("x" = some meaning of the card)	Example – Five of Cups (sample meaning = regret)
Self	this time period means "x" to me	this time period means regret to me
Other Person	this time period means "x" to this other person, from my point of view	this time period means regret to this other person, from my point of view
Group	this time period means "x" to the group as a whole	this time period means regret to the group as a whole
Area of Life	this time period means "x" within this area of life	this time period means regret within this area of life
Time Period	this related time period tends to mean "x" during the main subject time period	this time period tends to mean regret during the main subject time period
Problem	this time period means "x" within this problem this time period means "x" to someone involved in this problem	this time period means regret within this problem this time period means regret to someone involved in this problem
Choice	this time period means "x" when it comes to this choice this time period means "x" to me when it comes to this choice	this time period means regret when it comes to this choice this time period means regret to me when it comes to this choice
Project/Task	this time period means "x" within this project this time period means "x" to someone involved in this project	this time period means regret within this project this time period means regret to someone involved in this project
Event	this time period means "x" within this event this time period means "x" to someone involved in this event	this time period means regret within this event this time period means regret to someone involved in this event

POTENTIAL RELATED SUBJECT

Keywords:

central issue, core, crux, essence, focus, gist, heart of the matter, key, main idea, spirit, substance, theme

Description:

A potential related subject is a person or situation that exists as a possibility for the main subject. The potential subject is not actively involved at the time of a reading, but may become involved. It's waiting in the wings.

A card in this position shows a central or key feature of the potential subject from the point of view of the main subject. Potential subject cards help you become aware of people and situations before they impact you. Then you can encourage or discourage them as appropriate.

Potential Related Person

A potential related person is someone who may become meaningful to the main subject. A romantic new lover may step into your life (Knight of Cups). A potential donor may offer your group a generous gift (Star).

Reversed:

A potential person lacking some quality as far as the main subject is concerned. Someone who lacks discipline may become important to your family (reversed Nine of Pentacles). Your current manager may be replaced by someone less reliable (reversed King of Pentacles).

Flex-spread usage:

Far right position of the related person area, set slightly apart. The limit is one potential person per layout.

Table 9. POTENTIAL RELATED PERSON by Main Subject Type

If the Main Subject type is:	A Potential Related Person suggests: ("x" = some meaning of the card)	Example –Knight of Pentacles (sample meaning = stubbornness)
Self	a person may mean "x" to me at some point	a person may be stubborn with me at some point
Other Person	a person may mean "x" to the main subject person at some point, from my point of view	a person may be stubborn with the main subject person at some point, from my point of view
Group	a person may mean "x" to the group as a whole at some point	a person may be stubborn with the group as a whole at some point
Area of Life	a person may mean "x" to this area of life at some point	a person may be stubborn within this area of life at some point
Time Period	a person may mean "x" at some point during this time period	a person may be stubborn at some point during this time period
Problem	a person may mean "x" within this problem at some point a person may mean "x" to someone involved in this problem at some point	a person may be stubborn within this problem at some point a person may be stubborn with someone involved in this problem at some point
Choice	a person may mean "x" at some point when it comes to this choice a person may mean "x" to me at some point when it comes to this choice	a person may be stubborn at some point when it comes to this choice a person may be stubborn with me at some point when it comes to this choice
Project/Task	a person may mean "x" within this project at some point a person may mean "x" to someone involved in this project at some point	a person may be stubborn within this project at some point a person may be stubborn with someone involved in this project at some point
Event	a person may mean "x" within this event at some point a person may mean "x" to someone involved in this event at some point	a person may be stubborn within this event at some point a person may be stubborn with someone involved in this event at some point

Potential Related Situation

A potential related situation is a set of circumstances that may develop and become meaningful for the main subject. A situation may arise that alters your destiny (Wheel of Fortune). An event may occur that requires a sacrifice from your group (Ten of Swords). In a reading for your sister, an unexpected option may open up a new beginning for her (Fool).

Reversed:

A potential situation lacking some quality as far as the main subject is concerned. A challenge may arise that makes you feel a lack of confidence (reversed Ace of Wands). An unconventional event may occur during a certain time period (reversed Ten of Pentacles).

Flex-spread usage:

In the rightmost position in the related situation area, set slightly apart. The limit is one potential situation per layout.

Table 10. POTENTIAL RELATED SITUATION by Main Subject Type

If the Main Subject type is:	A Potential Related Situation suggests: ("x" = some meaning of the card)	Example – Five of Pentacles (sample meaning = hard times)
Self	a situation may mean "x" to me at some point	a situation may mean hard times to me at some point
Other Person	a situation may mean "x" to this other person at some point, from my point of view	a situation may mean hard times to this other person at some point, from my point of view
Group	a situation may mean "x" to the group as a whole at some point	a situation may mean hard times to the group as a whole at some point
Area of Life	a situation may mean "x" within this area of life at some point	a situation may mean hard times within this area of life at some point
Time Period	a situation may mean "x" at some point during this time period	a situation may mean hard times at some point during this time period
Problem	a situation may mean "x" within this problem at some point

a situation may mean "x" to someone involved in this problem at some point | a situation may mean hard times within this problem at some point

a situation may mean hard times to someone involved in this problem at some point |
| Choice | a situation may mean "x" at some point when it comes to this choice

a situation may mean "x" to me at some point when it comes to this choice | a situation may mean hard times at some point when it comes to this choice

a situation may mean hard times to me at some point when it comes to this choice |
| Project/Task | a situation may mean "x" within this project at some point

a situation may mean "x" to someone involved in this project at some point | a situation may mean hard times within this project at some point

a situation may mean hard times to someone involved in this project at some point |
| Event | a situation may mean "x" within this event at some point

a situation may mean "x" to someone involved in this event at some point | a situation may mean hard times within this event at some point

a situation may mean "x" to someone involved in this event at some point |

Guidance Position

Keywords:

advice, assistance, counsel, direction, enlightenment, help, opinion, point of view, recommendation, suggestion, wisdom

Description:

Guidance in a reading helps you understand the messages of the cards you draw. It offers insight that comes from the wise perspective of your inner guide.

Guidance is not a position in the usual sense. It's a card applied directly to a target position in a layout. A guidance card offers an opinion about the card in that position. This counsel comes from your inner guide to help you understand the target more deeply.

The meaning of a guidance card depends on the target. Guidance applied to a quality helps you assess the meaning of that quality for the main subject. Applied to a card in the quality "weak," the Seven of Wands as guidance suggests the main subject may be defensive about that weakness.

Guidance applied to a related subject card sheds light on that card's meaning for the main subject. It's hard to see the heartbreak of the Three of Swords in a potential person, but Strength as guidance lets you know you have the strength to deal with it.

Guidance applied to the main subject card covers not just that position, but the entire reading. It's an overall message from your inner guide about the main subject as a whole. For a reading about an event, the Ten of Cups suggests joy and peace may be guiding principles for the entire event.

Your response to guidance can help you assess its message. If you feel positive, the guidance is encouraging. If you feel negative, the guidance is a note of caution. In either case, your inner guide is always standing by, ready to support you with its wisdom.

Reversed:

The guidance suggests a lack of something is important in understanding the target card. The reversed Queen of Swords can show a lack of honesty when applied as guidance to a related person. The reversed Nine of Cups can imply a lack of satisfaction is in the air when applied to the environment position.

Flex-spread usage:

The lower right corner of a tipped target card.

Table 11. GUIDANCE for the Main Subject Position

If the main subject is:	the Guidance card suggests: ("x" = some meaning of guidance card)
Self	"x" helps me understand what is central or key about me
Other Person	"x" helps me understand what is central or key about this person
Area of Life	"x" helps me understand what is central or key about this area of my life
Time Period	"x" helps me understand what is central or key about this time period
Problem	"x" helps me understand what is central or key about this problem "x" helps me understand what is central or key about someone involved in this problem
Choice	"x" helps me understand what is central or key when it comes to this choice "x" helps me understand what is central or key about myself when it comes to this choice
Project/Task	"x" helps me understand what is central or key about this project "x" helps me understand what is central or key about someone involved in this project
Event	"x" helps me understand what is central or key about this event "x" helps me understand what is central or key about someone involved in this event

Table 12. GUIDANCE for Related and Potential Subject Positions

If the target position is:	the Guidance Card suggests: ("x" = meaning of guidance card)
Related Person	"x" helps me understand what this related person means to the main subject
Related Area of Life	"x" helps me understand what this related area of life means to the main subject
Related Situation	"x" helps me understand what this related situation means to the main subject
Related Time Period	"x" helps me understand what this related time period means to the main subject
Potential Person	"x" helps me understand what this potential person means to the main subject
Potential Situation	"x" helps me understand what this potential situation means to the main subject

Table 13. GUIDANCE for Quality Positions

If the target position is:	the Guidance Card suggests: ("x" = meaning of guidance card)
Active	"x" helps me understand what is active within the main subject
Avoiding	"x" helps me understand what the main subject is avoiding
Beginning	"x" helps me understand what is beginning within the main subject
Blocking	"x" helps me understand what is blocking within the main subject
Clearing	"x" helps me understand what is clearing the way within the main subject
Contributing to	"x" helps me understand what has contributed to the current state of the main subject
Disrupting	"x" helps me understand what is disrupting within the main subject

Table 13. GUIDANCE for Quality Positions, cont.

If the target position is:	the Guidance Card suggests: ("x" = meaning of guidance card)
Embracing	"x" helps me understand what the main subject is embracing
Ending	"x" helps me understand what is ending within the main subject
Enduring	"x" helps me understand what is enduring within the main subject
Environment	"x" helps me understand the environment surrounding the main subject
Heading toward	"x" helps me understand what the main subject is heading toward
Inactive	"x" helps me understand what is inactive within the main subject
Inside	"x" helps me understand what is going on inside the main subject
Known	"x" helps me understand what the main subject knows "x" helps me understand what is known about the main subject
New	"x" helps me understand what is new within the main subject
Old	"x" helps me understand what is old within the main subject
Outside	"x" helps me understand what is on the outside of the main subject
Potential	"x" helps me understand a potential within the main subject
Stabilizing	"x" helps me understand what is stabilizing within the main subject
Strong	"x" helps me understand what is strong within the main subject
Temporary	"x" helps me understand what is temporary within the main subject
Unknown	"x" helps me understand what the main subject doesn't know "x" helps me understand what is unknown about the main subject
Weak	"x" helps me understand what is weak within the main subject

QUALITY POSITIONS

Active

Keywords:

alive, animated, energized, engaged, enterprising, functioning, industrious, lively, occupied, spirited, vigorous, working

Description:

One meaning of "active" is to be energetic and lively. We're active when we're busy doing and going. The other meaning is functioning. Something is active when it's in operation. Either of these meanings can apply to the active position.

You may be actively responsible (Justice) in dealing with some duty. A pessimistic mood may be active on a project (Knight of Pentacles). A betrayal may become active on a certain day (Three of Swords).

Sometimes, a quality is dormant, but becomes "activated." You may become actively defiant after suffering a long time in silence (Seven of Wands). An active quality is engaged. It's having an impact for better or worse.

Reversed:

We normally think of a lack as something passive—a kind of void without energy. But a missing quality can be active in its own right. The spirit of an event may reflect an active lack of charm (reversed Knight of Wands).

Opposite Position:

inactive

Flex-spread usage:

To the right of the main subject position in the qualities area.

Table 14. ACTIVE Position by Main Subject Type

If the Main Subject is:	Active suggests: ("x" = some meaning of the card)	Example – Three of Wands (sample meaning = leadership)
Self	"x" is active within me	leadership is active within me
Other Person	"x" is active within this other person, from my point of view	leadership is active within this other person, from my point of view
Group	"x" is active within the group as a whole	leadership is active within the group as a whole
Area of Life	"x" is active within this area of my life	leadership is active within this area of my life
Time Period	"x" tends to be active during this time period	leadership tends to be active during this time period
Problem	"x" is active within this problem "x" is active within someone involved in this problem	leadership is active within this problem leadership is active within someone involved in this problem
Choice	"x" is active when it comes to this choice "x" is active within me when it comes to this choice	leadership is active when it comes to this choice leadership is active within me when it comes to this choice
Project/Task	"x" is active within this project "x" is active within someone involved in this project	leadership is active within this project leadership is active within someone involved in this project
Event	"x" is active within this event "x" is active within someone involved in this event	leadership is active within this event leadership is active within someone involved in this event

Avoiding

Keywords:

avoiding, denying, distancing from, dodging, evading, fearing, pushing away, refraining from, resisting, retreating from, shunning, steering clear of

Description:

To avoid means to deny or push away. If we fear or dislike something, we keep our distance. We try to pretend it's not true or doesn't exist. A card in avoiding shows something the main subject is resisting or denying. You may be avoiding your power (Magician). You may be refusing to be a martyr in some area of your life (Ten of Swords). A situation may involve someone who's denying rejection (Five of Pentacles).

Avoiding can be conscious or unconscious. You may realize you're avoiding—deliberately dodging a responsibility—or be unaware of it. Sometimes, we avoid out of disapproval. We feel negative, even antagonistic. At other times, we simply prefer not to face something that's difficult. Perhaps you're avoiding the need for hard control in dealing with a tough problem (Chariot).

Reversed:

The main subject is avoiding the fact that something is missing. The reality of this lack is what's being denied or pushed away. You may be avoiding a lack of recovery (reversed Six of Swords) or some lack of experience in yourself (reversed Queen of Swords).

Opposite Position:

embracing

Flex-spread usage:

To the left of the main subject position in the qualities area.

Table 15. AVOIDING Position by Main Subject Type

If the Main Subject is:	Avoiding suggests: ("x" = some meaning of the card)	Example – Strength (sample meaning = strength)
Self	I'm avoiding "x" in myself	I'm avoiding being strong
Other Person	this other person is avoiding "x," from my point of view	this other person is avoiding being strong, from my point of view
Group	the group as a whole is avoiding "x"	the group as a whole is avoiding being strong
Area of Life	avoiding "x" is a feature of this area of my life	avoiding being strong is a feature of this area of my life
Time Period	the tendency is to avoid "x" during this time period	the tendency is to avoid being strong during this time period
Problem	avoiding "x" is a feature of this problem someone involved in this problem is avoiding "x"	avoiding being strong is a feature of this problem someone involved in this problem is avoiding being strong
Choice	avoiding "x" is a feature of this choice I'm avoiding "x" when it comes to this choice	avoiding being strong is a feature of this choice I'm avoiding being strong when it comes to this choice
Project/Task	avoiding "x" is a feature of this project someone involved in this project is avoiding "x"	avoiding being strong is a feature of this project someone involved in this project is avoiding being strong
Event	avoiding "x" is a feature of this event someone involved in this event is avoiding "x"	avoiding being strong is a feature of this event someone involved in this event is avoiding being strong

Beginning

Keywords:

breaking ground, commencing, embarking on, entering, germinating, giving birth to, inaugurating, initiating, kicking off, launching, setting out, springing up, starting

Description:

Beginning is the action of starting or commencing. A card in beginning shows a quality just becoming available to the main subject. Perhaps a mystery is beginning in some area of your life (High Priestess). Losses may be starting to accrue (Five of Cups). A period of travel may be commencing for some project (Six of Swords). These are all beginnings.

A beginning quality can be brand new, or something reappearing. A beginning may be obvious or hidden. Sometimes a new seed has been planted, but the signs are not yet visible. A downfall may be in the works, but not yet apparent (Tower). When you're aware of beginnings, you have a chance to assist or reverse them.

Reversed:

The main subject is beginning to experience a lack of some quality. The quality is becoming less available. When a child leaves home, the need to mother may begin to lessen (reversed Empress).

Opposite Position:

ending

Flex-spread usage:

To the left of the main subject position in the qualities area.

Table 16. BEGINNING Position by Main Subject Type

If the Main Subject is:	Beginning suggests: ("x" = some meaning of the card)	Example – Six of Wands (sample meaning = triumph)
Self	"x" is beginning within me	feelings of triumph are beginning within me
Other Person	"x" is beginning within this other person, from my point of view	feelings of triumph are beginning within this other person, from my point of view
Group	"x" is beginning within the group as a whole	triumph is beginning within the group as a whole
Area of Life	"x" is beginning within this area of my life	triumph is beginning within this area of my life
Time Period	"x" tends to begin during this time period	triumph tends to begin during this time period
Problem	"x" is beginning within this problem "x" is beginning within someone involved in this problem	triumph is beginning within this problem feelings of triumph are beginning within someone involved in this problem
Choice	"x" is beginning when it comes to this choice "x" is beginning within me when it comes to this choice	triumph is beginning when it comes to this choice feelings of triumph are beginning within me when it comes to this choice
Project/Task	"x" is beginning within this project "x" is beginning within someone involved in this project	triumph is beginning within this project feelings of triumph are beginning within someone involved in this project
Event	"x" is beginning within this event "x" is beginning within someone involved in this event	triumph is beginning within this event feelings of triumph are beginning within someone involved in this event

Blocking

Keywords:

discouraging, frustrating, hindering, holding back, impeding, limiting, obstructing, opposing, preventing, restraining, retarding, slowing, thwarting

Description:

Blocking energy slows and impedes. It keeps things from moving forward. A card in blocking shows some quality obstructing progress for the main subject. You may be feeling blocked by some fear (Moon). Someone may be feeling hampered by their hot temper (Knight of Wands). Restrictions may be creating obstacles in a situation (Eight of Swords).

Usually blocking energy seems negative. Our impulse is to remove or neutralize whatever is standing in our way. But sometimes restraint is welcome. If events are moving forward too quickly, some limits may be helpful. Guilty feelings keep you from doing something you may regret (Nine of Swords). Before you remove the blocks in your life, be sure they are truly hindering you.

Reversed:

A block or obstruction due to a lack of some quality. Progress is slow because something is missing. If the element is introduced, conditions may move forward. A lack of education may be holding you back in your career (reversed Hierophant).

Opposite Position:

clearing

Flex-spread usage:

To the left of the main subject position in the qualities area.

Table 17. BLOCKING Position by Main Subject Type

If the Main Subject is:	Blocking suggests: ("x" = some meaning of the card)	Example – Four of Cups (sample meaning = apathy)
Self	"x" is blocking within me	my apathy is blocking within me
Other Person	"x" is blocking within this other person, from my point of view	apathy is blocking within this other person, from my point of view
Group	"x" is blocking within the group as a whole	apathy is blocking within the group as a whole
Area of Life	"x" is blocking within this area of my life	apathy is blocking within this area of my life
Time Period	"x" tends to be blocking during this time period	apathy tends to be blocking during this time period
Problem	"x" is blocking within this problem "x" is blocking within someone involved in this problem	apathy is blocking within this problem apathy is blocking within someone involved in this problem
Choice	"x" is blocking when it comes to this choice my "x" is blocking within me when it comes to this choice	apathy is blocking when it comes to this choice my apathy is blocking within me when it comes to this choice
Project/Task	"x" is blocking within this project "x" is blocking within someone involved in this project	apathy is blocking within this project apathy is blocking within someone involved in this project
Event	"x" is blocking within this event "x" is blocking within someone involved in this event	apathy is blocking within this event apathy is blocking within someone involved in this event

Clearing

Keywords:

accelerating, aiding, assisting, expediting, fostering, freeing, furthering, getting rid of, hastening, helping, lending a hand to, opening, promoting, removing, unblocking

Description:

Clearing means removing obstacles. When you clear something away, you get rid of it so you're free to move forward. A card in clearing shows a quality helping the main subject to advance. It aids and assists. A new enthusiasm may be helping you succeed in a task (Ace of Wands). A wise and caring friend may be lending a hand (King of Cups). Acclaim may be clearing the way for you in your work (Six of Wands).

Clearing can create a new path or expedite an existing one. It can be recognized as helpful or destructive, depending on the path. Sometimes, inexorable forces clear away the old even when you're not ready (Death). A clearing quality can hurry you down a path you might not take if it weren't so easy. Be sure of the consequences before you encourage a clearing.

Reversed:

A lack of some quality is clearing. The path forward is free because something is missing. A lack of weariness can help you handle your many tasks (reversed Eight of Cups).

Opposite Position:

blocking

Flex-spread usage:

To the right of the main subject position in the qualities area.

Table 18. CLEARING Position by Main Subject Type

If the Main Subject is:	Clearing suggests ("x" = some meaning of the card)	Example – Page of Cups (sample meaning = being intimate)
Self	"x" is clearing the way for me	being intimate is clearing the way for me
Other Person	"x" is clearing the way for this other person, from my point of view	being intimate is clearing the way for this other person, from my point of view
Group	"x" is clearing the way for the group as a whole	being intimate is clearing the way for the group as a whole
Area of Life	"x" is clearing the way within this area of my life	being intimate is clearing the way within this area of my life
Time Period	"x" tends to clear the way during this time period	being intimate tends to clear the way during this time period
Problem	"x" is clearing the way within this problem "x" is clearing the way for someone involved in this problem	being intimate is clearing the way within this problem being intimate is clearing the way for someone involved in this problem
Choice	"x" is clearing the way when it comes to this choice "x" is clearing the way for me when it comes to this choice	being intimate is clearing the way when it comes to this choice being intimate is clearing the way for me when it comes to this choice
Project/Task	"x" is clearing the way within this project "x" is clearing the way for someone involved in this project	being intimate is clearing the way within this project being intimate is clearing the way for someone involved in this project
Event	"x" is clearing the way within this event "x" is clearing the way for someone involved in this event	being intimate is clearing the way within this event being intimate is clearing the way for someone involved in this event

Contributing to

Keywords:

bringing about, causing, creating, generating, impacting, inciting, inducing, influencing, inspiring, leading to, precipitating, producing

Description:

Contributing to identifies a quality that has led directly to the current state of the main subject. It shows something influencing present conditions. You may be enjoying abundance because of earlier enterprise (King of Pentacles). A problem may be worsening because those involved have been defensive (Nine of Wands).

Contributing to is related to the past. We think of the past as causing the present, but that's not exactly true. It's the energies you carry from the past into the present that make the difference. Memories of past hard times can make you overly cautious (Five of Pentacles).

A cause implies a single, fixed effect. Contributing to shows an important influence, but perhaps just one among many. The success of an event depends on wholehearted effort, but not totally (Queen of Wands). A contributing quality can be major or minor, but it's always worth knowing about.

Reversed:

A lack of some quality is contributing to the current state of the main subject. A shortage has led to present conditions. A lack of options can create a feeling of being stuck (reversed Seven of Cups).

Opposite Position:

heading toward

Flex-spread usage:

To the left of the main subject position in the qualities area.

Table 19. CONTRIBUTING TO Position by Main Subject Type

If the Main Subject is:	Contributing to suggests: ("x" = some meaning of the card)	Example – Nine of Pentacles (sample meaning = self-reliance)
Self	"x" has contributed to my current state	my self-reliance has contributed to my current state
Other Person	"x" has contributed to this other person's current state, from my point of view	self-reliance has contributed to this person's current state, from my point of view
Group	"x" has contributed to the current state of the group as a whole	self-reliance has contributed to the current state of the group as a whole
Area of Life	"x" has contributed to this area of my life	self-reliance has contributed to this area of my life
Time Period	"x" has contributed to the conditions during this time period	self-reliance has contributed to the conditions during this time period
Problem	"x" has contributed to the current state of this problem "x" has contributed to the current state of someone involved in this problem	self-reliance has contributed to the current state of this problem self-reliance has contributed to the current state of someone involved in this problem
Choice	"x" has contributed to the current state of this choice "x" has contributed to my current state when it comes to this choice	self-reliance has contributed to the current state of this choice self-reliance has contributed to my current state when it comes to this choice
Project/Task	"x" has contributed to the current state of this project "x" has contributed to the current state of someone involved in this project	self-reliance has contributed to the current state of this project self-reliance has contributed to the current state of someone involved in this project
Event	"x" has contributed to the current state of this event "x" has contributed to the current state of someone involved in this event	self-reliance has contributed to the current state of this event self-reliance has contributed to the current state of someone involved in this event

Disrupting

Keywords:

changing, destabilizing, disconcerting, disordering, disturbing, overturning, shaking, shifting, shuffling, unbalancing, upsetting, unsettling

Description:

A disrupting force causes change. It shakes up the status quo. A card in disrupting shows some quality that is upsetting the existing order for the main subject. You may be feeling disrupted by the need to let go (Hanged Man). Someone obsessive may be disrupting progress at work (Knight of Pentacles). A quick action may be disrupting an event (Eight of Wands).

Sometimes a disrupting force is destructive. An open dishonor can destroy trust and good will (Five of Swords). At other times, a disruption brings welcome change. It may be unsettling, but it creates an opportunity for new growth. A powerful revelation can have this effect (Tower). Some disruptions are strong, some mild. Whether or not one is helpful depends on all the conditions of the moment.

Reversed:

A lack of some quality is disrupting. Its absence is having a destabilizing effect. An organization can lose its bearings when a charismatic leader steps down (reversed King of Wands).

Opposite Position:

stabilizing

Flex-spread usage:

To the right of the main subject position in the qualities area.

Table 20. DISRUPTING Position by Main Subject Type

If the Main Subject is:	Disrupting suggests ("x" = some meaning of the card)	Example – Ace of Wands (sample meaning = courage)
Self	my "x" is disrupting within me	courage is disrupting within me
Other Person	"x" is disrupting within this other person, from my point of view	courage is disrupting within this other person, from my point of view
Group	"x" is disrupting within the group as a whole	courage is disrupting within the group as a whole
Area of Life	"x" is disrupting within this area of my life	courage is disrupting within this area of my life
Time Period	"x" tends to be disrupting during this time period	courage tends to be disrupting during this time period
Problem	"x" is disrupting within this problem "x" is disrupting within someone involved in this problem	courage is disrupting within this problem courage is disrupting within someone involved in this problem
Choice	"x" is disrupting when it comes to this choice "x" is disrupting within me when it comes to this choice	courage is disrupting when it comes to this choice courage is disrupting within me when it comes to this choice
Project/Task	"x" is disrupting within this project "x" is disrupting within someone involved in this project	courage is disrupting within this project courage is disrupting within someone involved in this project
Event	"x" is disrupting within this event "x" is disrupting within someone involved in this event	courage is disrupting within this event courage is disrupting within someone involved in this event

Embracing

Keywords:

admiring, approving, believing in, desiring, endorsing, hoping for, honoring, liking, praising, supporting, valuing, wanting, welcoming, wishing for

Description:

Embracing means to enfold within or to wrap your arms around. When we embrace something, we have warm, positive feelings toward it. We want to make it part of ourselves. A card in embracing shows some quality valued by the main subject. You may be embracing your psychic ability (Queen of Cups). A group may be valuing a lone-wolf style (Seven of Swords). Some choice may involve embracing competition (Five of Wands).

The positive regard can range from simple acceptance to eager support. The quality may be possessed by the main subject, or just desired. You can even embrace undesirable qualities—those you know are not worthwhile or helpful. A person may hold on to bondage (Devil) even when freedom is offered.

Reversed:

The main subject is embracing the lack of some quality. Not having something is what's desired. You may be embracing a lack of connection to someone else (reversed Two of Cups).

Opposite Position:

avoiding

Flex-spread usage:

To the right of the main subject position in the qualities area.

Table 21. EMBRACING Position by Main Subject Type

If the Main Subject is:	Embracing suggests: ("x" = some meaning of the card)	Example – Moon (sample meaning = illusions)
Self	I'm embracing "x" within myself	I'm embracing illusions about myself
Other Person	this other person is embracing "x," from my point of view	this other person is embracing illusions, from my point of view
Group	the group as a whole is embracing "x"	the group as a whole is embracing illusions
Area of Life	embracing "x" is a feature of this area of my life	embracing illusions is a feature of this area of my life
Time Period	the tendency is to embrace "x" during this time period	the tendency is to embrace illusions during this time period
Problem	embracing "x" is a feature of this problem someone involved in this problem is embracing "x"	embracing illusions is a feature of this problem someone involved in this problem is embracing illusions
Choice	embracing "x" is a feature when it comes to this choice I'm embracing "x" when it comes to this choice	embracing illusions is a feature when it comes to this choice I'm embracing illusions when it comes to this choice
Project/Task	embracing "x" is a feature of this project someone involved in this project is embracing "x"	embracing illusions is a feature of this project someone involved in this project is embracing illusions
Event	embracing "x" is a feature of this event someone involved in this event is embracing "x"	embracing illusions is a feature of this event someone involved in this event is embracing illusions

Ending

Keywords:

ceasing, closing, concluding, expiring, fading, finishing, leaving, moving away, passing on, stopping, terminating, winding up

Description:

Our lives are filled with energies that rise and fall in strength and importance. Ending represents the falling side. Something is moving away or drawing to a close. A card in ending shows a quality that has been active, but is now fading. You may be leaving your family (Ten of Cups). Some choice may involve setting aside self-interest to end a fight (Five of Swords). Someone in your life may be letting go of control (Four of Pentacles).

An ending may be just starting or quite advanced. You can welcome a down-ward trend or resist it. At a project's end, you may be glad or sad that the hard work is over (Knight of Pentacles). Sometimes knowing an ending is in progress can help you decide how to deal with it.

Reversed:

A lack is ending. A quality was missing, but now it's becoming available. Perhaps you've had few options, but now doors are opening (reversed Seven of Cups). Your lack of choice is ending.

Opposite Position:

beginning

Flex-spread usage:

To the right of the main subject position in the qualities area.

Table 22. ENDING Position by Main Subject Type

If the Main Subject is:	Ending suggests: ("x" = some meaning of the card)	Example – Queen of Pentacles (sample meaning = nurturing)
Self	"x" is ending within me	nurturing is ending within me
Other Person	"x" is ending within this other person, from my point of view	nurturing is ending within this other person, from my point of view
Group	"x" is ending within the group as a whole	nurturing is ending within the group as a whole
Area of Life	"x" is ending within this area of my life	nurturing is ending within this area of my life
Time Period	"x" tends to end during this time period	nurturing tends to end during this time period
Problem	"x" is ending within this problem "x" is ending within someone involved in this problem	nurturing is ending within this problem nurturing is ending within someone involved in this problem
Choice	"x" is ending when it comes to this choice "x" is ending within me when it comes to this choice	nurturing is ending when it comes to this choice nurturing is ending within me when it comes to this choice
Project/Task	"x" is ending within this project "x" is ending within someone involved in this project	nurturing is ending within this project nurturing is ending within someone involved in this project
Event	"x" is ending within this event "x" is ending within someone involved in this event	nurturing is ending within this event nurturing is ending within someone involved in this event

Enduring

Keywords:

continuing, chronic, durable, lasting, long-lived, long-term, permanent, persistent, prolonged, protracted, surviving, unfading

Description:

Enduring means lasting over time. Something is enduring if it has the deep roots and strength to persist. A card in enduring shows a quality that has staying power. You may be glad to learn a relationship is enduring (Lovers). Other times, you may wish for less permanence, as with a chronic illness (Five of Pentacles).

Sometimes an enduring quality has existed for a long time and is going to continue. Other times a quality is new, but still durable. A truce between warring parties may be a lasting one (Two of Cups). A new choice may promise long-term creative possibilities (Page of Wands). Although nothing lasts forever, an enduring quality is tough enough to survive.

Reversed:

Some lack is enduring. A quality has been absent or scarce for a long time. A long-term lack of leadership can create problems in a group (reversed Three of Wands).

Opposite Position:

temporary

Flex-spread usage:

To the left of the main subject position in the qualities area.

Table 23. ENDURING Position by Main Subject Type

If the Main Subject is:	Enduring suggests: ("x" = some meaning of the card)	Example – World (sample meaning = accomplishment)
Self	"x" is enduring within me	accomplishment is enduring within me
Other Person	"x" is enduring within this other person, from my point of view	accomplishment is enduring within this other person, from my point of view
Group	"x" is enduring within the group as a whole	accomplishment is enduring within the group as a whole
Area of Life	"x" is enduring within this area of my life	accomplishment is enduring within this area of my life
Time Period	"x" tends to endure during this time period	accomplishment tends to endure during this time period
Problem	"x" is enduring within this problem	accomplishment is enduring within this problem
	"x" is ending within someone involved in this problem	accomplishment is enduring within someone involved in this problem
Choice	"x" is enduring when it comes to this choice	accomplishment is enduring when it comes to this choice
	"x" is enduring within me when it comes to this choice	accomplishment is enduring within me when it comes to this choice
Project/Task	"x" is enduring within this project	accomplishment is enduring within this project
	"x" is enduring within someone involved in this project	accomplishment is enduring within someone involved in this project
Event	"x" is enduring within this event	accomplishment is enduring within this event
	"x" is enduring within someone involved in this event	accomplishment is enduring within someone involved in this event

Environment

Keywords:

environment, atmosphere, surroundings, milieu, climate, ambience, setting, outer conditions

Description:

Environment describes the atmosphere or conditions surrounding the main subject of a reading. It shows what is completely "outside" the subject, yet still impacting it. Often a card in this position conveys the general mood or climate. The mood around you may be joyful (Ten of Cups) or anguished (Nine of Swords). The climate of an event may be free (Four of Wands) or restrictive (Eight of Swords).

Sometimes environment shows an event or activity going on around the main subject, such as an ending (Death) or decision (Justice). It can point out some feature of the environment that's not yet obvious. Perhaps someone is planning to run away, but hasn't left yet (Seven of Swords). The environment position helps you stay aware of your surroundings.

Reversed:

The environment lacks some quality. Something is missing in the atmosphere surrounding the main subject. A project may be struggling because the people around it lack knowledge of its goals (reversed Six of Pentacles.)

Opposite Position:

Flex-spread usage:

Directly above the main subject position in the qualities area.

Table 24. ENVIRONMENT Position by Main Subject Type

If the Main Subject is:	Environment suggests: ("x" = some meaning of the card)	Example – Three of Swords (sample meaning = loneliness)
Self	the environment surrounding me is "x"	the environment surrounding me is lonely
Other Person	the environment surrounding this other person is "x," from my point of view	the environment surrounding this other person is lonely, from my point of view
Group	the environment surrounding the group as a whole is "x"	the environment surrounding the group as a whole is lonely
Area of Life	the environment surrounding this area of my life is "x"	the environment surrounding this area of my life is lonely
Time Period	the environment surrounding this time period is "x"	the environment surrounding this time period is lonely
Problem	the environment surrounding this problem is "x" the environment surrounding someone involved in this problem is "x"	the environment surrounding this problem is lonely the environment surrounding someone involved in this problem is lonely
Choice	the environment surrounding this choice is "x" the environment surrounding me is "x" when it comes to this choice	the environment surrounding this choice is lonely the environment surrounding me is lonely when it comes to this choice
Project/Task	the environment surrounding this project is "x" the environment surrounding someone involved in this project is "x"	the environment surrounding this project is lonely the environment surrounding someone involved in this project is lonely
Event	the environment surrounding this event is "x" the environment surrounding someone involved in this event is "x"	the environment surrounding this event is lonely the environment surrounding someone involved in this event is lonely

Heading Toward

Keywords:

bound for, going toward, leading toward, moving in the direction of, pointing toward, tending toward, verging on

Description:

Heading toward means going in a certain direction. It implies taking a definite path. A card in this position shows a probable outcome for the main subject. It's a projected result based on the subject's state at the time of the reading. You may be heading toward discord and conflict (Five of Swords). A problem may be tending toward a loving resolution (Page of Cups).

An outcome position is one of the most popular in the tarot. People always want to know what will happen in the future. But "outcome" implies a fixed result. Heading toward suggests only a direction. It shows you where you're likely to go based on present conditions so you can work with your future productively.

Heading toward can be a warning. Knowing a relationship is heading toward heartbreak (Three of Swords) can help you make needed changes. Heading toward can also hold out hope. You may embrace a choice heading toward joy (Ten of Cups).

Reversed:

The main subject is heading toward a lack of some quality. Current conditions are leading to a shortage. A move you're considering may be heading you toward a loss of community (reversed Three of Cups).

Opposite Position:

contributing to

Flex-spread usage:

To the right of the main subject position in the qualities area.

Table 25. HEADING TOWARD Position by Main Subject Type

If the Main Subject is:	Heading toward suggests: ("x" = some meaning of the card)	Example – Eight of Cups (sample quality = weariness)
Self	I'm heading toward "x"	I'm heading toward weariness
Other Person	this other person is heading toward "x," from my point of view	this other person's heading toward weariness, from my point of view
Group	the group as a whole is heading toward "x"	the group as a whole is heading toward weariness
Area of Life	this area of my life is heading toward "x" I'm heading toward "x" in this area of my life	this area of my life is heading toward weariness I'm heading toward weariness in this area of my life
Time Period	conditions during this time period are heading toward "x"	conditions during this time period are heading toward weariness
Problem	this problem is heading toward "x" someone involved in this problem is heading toward "x"	this problem is heading toward weariness someone involved in this problem is heading toward weariness
Choice	this choice is heading toward "x" I'm heading toward "x" when it comes to this choice	this choice is heading toward weariness I'm heading toward weariness when it comes to this choice
Project/Task	this project is heading toward "x" someone involved in this project is heading toward "x"	this project is heading toward weariness someone involved in this project is heading toward weariness
Event	this event is heading toward "x" someone involved in this event is heading toward "x"	this event is heading toward weariness someone involved in this event is heading toward weariness

Inactive

Keywords:

idle, inoperative, low-key, on hold, on the shelf, on the sidelines, out of service, unused

Description:

Something is inactive when it's idle. It's out of service for the moment, but could be restarted. A card in inactive shows some quality that's normally present, but not in operation for the moment. Perhaps your strong, romantic feelings are on hold (Knight of Cups). You may be enjoying a time-out from your usual job struggle (Ten of Wands). Normal regulations may be suspended for an event (Emperor).

An inactive quality is often in the background. It exists, but there's not much energy in it for the moment. A friendship is inactive in this sense when both parties are busy elsewhere (Three of Cups). We can feel glad or concerned when a quality is inactive depending on its effects.

Reversed:

A quality that's normally absent, but for the moment, is active. In other words, the lack is inactive! You may normally avoid introspection, but after being criticized, you begin to think about your behavior (reversed Hermit).

Opposite Position:

active

Flex-spread usage:

To the left of the main subject position in the qualities area.

Table 26. INACTIVE Position by Main Subject Type

If the Main Subject is:	Inactive suggests: ("x" = some meaning of the card)	Example – Six of Swords (sample meaning = recovery)
Self	"x" is inactive within me	recovery is inactive within me
Other Person	"x" is inactive within this other person, from my point of view	recovery is inactive within this other person, from my point of view
Group	"x" is inactive within the group as a whole	recovery is inactive within the group as a whole
Area of Life	"x" is inactive within this area of my life	recovery is inactive within this area of my life
Time Period	"x" tends to be inactive during this time period	recovery tends to be inactive during this time period
Problem	"x" is inactive within this problem "x" is inactive within someone involved in this problem	recovery is inactive within this problem recovery is inactive within someone involved in this problem
Choice	"x" is inactive when it comes to this choice "x" is inactive within me when it comes to this choice	recovery is inactive when it comes to this choice recovery is inactive within me when it comes to this choice
Project/Task	"x" is inactive within this project "x" is inactive within someone involved in this project	recovery is inactive within this project recovery is inactive within someone involved in this project
Event	"x" is inactive within this event "x" is inactive within someone involved in this event	recovery is inactive within this event recovery is inactive within someone involved in this event

Inside

Keywords:

below the surface, inconspicuous, inner, inner face, interior, internal, out of view, unapparent, hidden, within

Description:

Sometimes outward appearances belie inner reality. A card in inside shows what's going on below the surface of the main subject. It offers a glimpse into that interior. You may feel excited (Four of Wands) despite your calm demeanor. An idea may seem far-fetched, but actually be practical (Ace of Pentacles). The inside position looks past the obvious to the deeper quality within. For a moment the veil is lifted.

For people, inside often shows thoughts, feelings, or intentions. Someone may seem warm and friendly, but be unfeeling on the inside (Knight of Swords). In a situation, inside hints at the inner workings. A project wildly disorganized on the outside may have internal balance (Temperance). Sometimes, inside and outside are the same. In this case, a card in inside will be consistent with other cards in a reading.

Reversed:

A lack of some quality within the main subject. Something is missing on the inside. There may be a lack of integration within a project (reversed World).

Opposite Position:

outside

Flex-spread usage:

To the left of the main subject position in the qualities area.

Table 27. INSIDE Position by Main Subject Type

If the Main Subject is:	Inside suggests: ("x" = some meaning of the card)	Example – Seven of Pentacles (sample meaning = direction change)
Self	"x" is going on inside me	a direction change is going on inside me
Other Person	"x" is going on inside this other person, from my point of view	a direction change is going on inside this other person, from my point of view
Group	"x" is going on inside the group as a whole	a direction change is going on inside the group as a whole
Area of Life	"x" is going on inside this area of my life	a direction change is going on inside this area of my life
Time Period	"x" tends to be going on inside during this time period	a direction change tends to be going on inside during this time period
Problem	"x" is going on inside this problem	a direction change is going on inside this problem
	"x" is going on inside someone involved in this problem	a direction change is going on inside someone involved in this problem
Choice	"x" is going on inside when it comes to this choice	a direction change is going on inside when it comes to this choice
	"x" is going on inside me when it comes to this choice	a direction change is going on inside me when it comes to this choice
Project/Task	"x" is going on inside this project	a direction change is going on inside this project
	"x" is going on inside someone involved in this project	a direction change is going on inside someone involved in this project
Event	"x" is going on inside this event	a direction change is going on inside this event
	"x" is going on inside someone involved in this event	a direction change is going on inside someone involved in this event

Known

Keywords:

acquainted with, aware of, comprehended, conscious of, familiar, informed of, out in the open, perceived, public, realized, recognized, understood

Description:

To know is to be aware of. Before something can be known, it must first be revealed. A card in known can show something brought to light for or about the main subject. It's no longer a secret. A hidden dishonor may be exposed about a group (Seven of Swords).

Knowing can also mean accepting as true. A card in known can show something that's "common knowledge" to or about the main subject. It's recognized as fact. You may know a direction change is planned for an event (Seven of Pentacles). Someone who's known to be ethical may mediate a problem (King of Swords).

Finally, knowing can imply understanding. You can be exposed to something and yet not know it. You must first comprehend its essence, perhaps at many levels, before you know it deeply. You may know someone is innocent despite appearances (Six of Cups).

Reversed:

A lack of something is what is known. There's agreement that some quality is missing. A start-up company may know there's a shortage of resources to get the job done (reversed Six of Pentacles).

Opposite Position:

unknown

Flex-spread usage:

To the right of the main subject position in the qualities area.

Table 28. KNOWN Position by Main Subject Type

If the Main Subject is:	Known suggests: ("x" = some meaning of the card)	Example – Eight of Wands (sample meaning = news)
Self	I know "x" "x" is known about me	I know news news is known about me
Other Person	this other person knows "x," from my point of view "x" is known about this other person, from my point of view	this other person knows news, from my point of view news is known about this other person, from my point of view
Group	the group knows "x" "x" is known about the group	the group knows news news is known about the group
Area of Life	"x" is known within this area of my life "x" is known about this area of my life	news is known within this area of my life news is known about this area of my life
Time Period	"x" tends to be known during this time period	news tends to be known during this time period
Problem	"x" is known in relation to this problem someone involved in this problem knows "x" "x" is known about someone involved in this problem	news is known in relation to this problem someone involved in this problem knows news news is known about someone involved in this problem
Choice	"x" is known when it comes to this choice I know "x" when it comes to this choice "x" is known about me when it comes to this choice	news is known when it comes to this choice I know news when it comes to this choice news is known about me when it comes to this choice
Project/ Task	"x" is known about this project someone involved in this project knows "x" "x" is known about someone involved in this project	news is known about this project someone involved in this project knows news news is known about someone involved in this project
Event	"x" is known about this event someone involved in this event knows "x" "x" is known about someone involved in this event	news is known about this event someone involved in this event knows news news is known about someone involved in this event

New

Keywords:

different, fresh, just out, novel, unfamiliar, unique, unusual, untested, untried, unused

Description:

New is different. A card in new shows a quality that's novel or unfamiliar for the main subject. You may be enjoying a new burst of creative energy (King of Wands). A loss may be a new experience for a team (Five of Cups).

The new can appear quietly and go unnoticed. Or, it can arrive suddenly and full-blown. Without warning, all the rules are different. An unexpected choice may offer a chance to enjoy new prosperity (Page of Pentacles). The new is also untested. You don't know whether it will bring wanted or unwanted change. Going through a rebirth is a new experience that can bring surprises (Judgment). No matter what, the new always stirs things up.

Reversed:

A lack of some quality is new for the main subject. The quality has been present, but now it's gone and that's new. A lack of avoiding may be a new development for you (reversed Two of Swords).

Opposite Position:

old

Flex-spread usage:

To the right of the main subject position in the qualities area.

Table 29. NEW Position by Main Subject Type

If the Main Subject is:	New suggests: ("x" = some meaning of the card)	Example – Nine of Cups (sample meaning = satisfaction)
Self	"x" is new within me	satisfaction is new within me
Other Person	"x" is new within this other person, from my point of view	satisfaction is new within this other person, from my point of view
Group	"x" is new within the group as a whole	satisfaction is new within the group as a whole
Area of Life	"x" is new within this area of my life	satisfaction is new within this area of my life
Time Period	"x" tends to be new during this time period	satisfaction tends to be new during this time period
Problem	"x" is new within this problem "x" is new within someone involved in this problem	satisfaction is new within this problem satisfaction is new within someone involved in this problem
Choice	"x" is new when it comes to this choice "x" is new within me when it comes to this choice	satisfaction is new when it comes to this choice satisfaction is new within me when it comes to this choice
Project/Task	"x" is new within this project "x" is new within someone involved in this project	satisfaction is new within this project satisfaction is new within someone involved in this project
Event	"x" is new within this event "x" is new within someone involved in this event	satisfaction is new within this event satisfaction is new within someone involved in this event

Old

Keywords:

customary, traditional, usual, classic, time-honored, behind the times, dated, obsolete, old-fashioned, old hat, out of date, passé, stale, timeworn, tired

Description:

The old is something that's been around for a long time. A card in old can show a quality that's endured and persisted. You may have always been introverted (Knight of Cups)—it's "old" to you.

The old can also be time-honored—valued because of its age and worth. An old friend may be loved for his or her steady, reliable support (King of Pentacles). Finally, the old can be something that's outlived its usefulness. It's stale and tired. A period of rest may be welcome for a time, but it gets old if it lasts too long (Four of Swords). Sometimes, you can honor and appreciate what's old, but at other times, you need to make room for the new.

Reversed:

A long-standing lack of some quality. You may have gone without affluence for a long time (reversed Ten of Pentacles). Doing without has been the norm.

Opposite Position:

new

Flex-spread usage:

To the left of the main subject position in the qualities area.

Table 30. OLD Position by Main Subject Type

If the Main Subject is:	Old suggests ("x" = some meaning of the card)	Example – Ace of Pentacles (sample meaning = practicality)
Self	"x" is old within me	being practical is old within me
Other Person	"x" is old within this other person, from my point of view	being practical is old within this other person, from my point of view
Group	"x" is old within the group as a whole	being practical is old within the group as a whole
Area of Life	"x" is old within this area of my life	being practical is old within this area of my life
Time Period	"x" tends to be old during this time	being practical tends to be old during this time
Problem	"x" is old within this problem "x" is old within someone involved in this problem	being practical is old within this problem being practical is old within someone involved in this problem
Choice	"x" is old when it comes to this choice "x" is old within me when it comes to this choice	being practical is old when it comes to this choice being practical is old within me when it comes to this choice
Project/Task	"x" is old within this project "x" is old within someone involved in this project	being practical is old within this project being practical is old within someone involved in this project
Event	"x" is old within this event "x" is old within someone involved in this event	being practical is old within this event being practical is old within someone involved in this event

Outside

Keywords:

apparent, conspicuous, displayed, exterior, external, obvious, on view, ostensible, outer, outward face, presented, shown, surface, without

Description:

A card in outside shows the outer face of the main subject—its external appearance. This includes the physical, but goes beyond it as well. Sometimes outside shows a style of interacting with the outer world. You may be direct and authoritative with others (Knight of Swords). Outside can also show how the main subject is coming across to others. An event may be perceived from without as a call for justice (Ace of Swords).

Sometimes, outside describes what seems to be true on the surface, even though it doesn't match what's inside. A group may show faith outwardly (Fool), but harbor doubts within. Compare a card in outside with others to see if they're consistent. If not, then appearances may not be the whole story.

Reversed:

An outer lack of some quality. The main subject appears to be without the quality from the outside. A stern judge can appear to lack compassion on the surface (reversed Strength).

Opposite Position:

inside

Flex-spread usage:

To the right of the main subject position in the qualities area.

Table 31. OUTSIDE Position by Main Subject Type

If the Main Subject is:	Outside suggests: ("x" = some meaning of the card)	Example – Hierophant (sample meaning = conformity)
Self	I'm "x" on the outside	I'm conforming on the outside
Other Person	this other person is "x" on the outside, from my point of view	this other person is conforming on the outside, from my point of view
Group	the group as a whole is "x" on the outside	the group as a whole is conforming on the outside
Area of Life	this area of my life is "x" on the outside	this area of my life is conforming on the outside
Time Period	"x" tends to be on the outside during this time period	conforming tends to be on the outside during this time period
Problem	this problem is "x" on the outside	this problem is conforming on the outside
	someone involved in this problem is "x" on the outside	someone involved in this problem is conforming on the outside
Choice	"x" is on the outside when it comes to this choice	conforming is on the outside when it comes to this choice
	I'm "x" on the outside when it comes to this choice	I'm conforming on the outside when it comes to this choice
Project/Task	this project is "x" on the outside	this project is conforming on the outside
	someone involved in this project is "x" on the outside	someone involved in this project is conforming on the outside
Event	this event is "x" on the outside	this event is conforming on the outside
	someone involved in this event is "x" on the outside	someone involved in this event is conforming on the outside

Potential (Quality)

Keywords:

dormant, in the wings, latent, possible, waiting, undeveloped, unexposed, unexpressed, unmanifested, unrealized

Description:

A potential quality is one that exists as a possibility. It's dormant, waiting to be expressed. A card in this position shows something available to the main subject, but not yet realized. You may have a hidden reserve of patience (Strength). Someone involved in an event may be a potential diplomat (King of Cups). A potential can be an item or activity. A reward may be a possibility in a certain situation (Seven of Pentacles).

Some potentials are unsuspected. A creative opportunity may exist that you're not aware of (Ace of Wands). Others potentials are known, but considered undesirable. An unpleasant disagreement may be about to erupt in some area of your life (Five of Wands). Knowing the potentials that exist can help you encourage or discourage them as appropriate.

Reversed:

A potential for the lack of something. The quality exists now, but could be reduced or lost. Goodwill could potentially be lost or destroyed in a situation (reversed Six of Cups).

Opposite Position:

Flex-spread usage:

Directly below the main subject position in the qualities area.

Table 32. POTENTIAL (Quality) Position by Main Subject Type

If the **Main Subject is:**	Potential Quality suggests: ("x" = some meaning of the card)	Example – Sun (sample meaning = greatness)
Self	"x" is a potential within me	greatness is a potential within me
Other Person	"x" is a potential within this other person, from my point of view	greatness is a potential within this other person, from my point of view
Group	"x" is a potential within the group	greatness is a potential within the group
Area of Life	"x" is a potential within this area of my life	greatness is a potential within this area of my life
Time Period	"x" is a potential during this time period	greatness is a potential during this time period
Problem	"x" is a potential within this problem "x" is a potential within someone involved in this problem	greatness is a potential within this problem greatness is a potential within someone involved in this problem
Choice	"x" is a potential when it comes to this choice "x" is a potential within me when it comes to this choice	greatness is a potential when it comes to this choice greatness is a potential within me when it comes to this choice
Project/Task	"x" is a potential within this project "x" is a potential within someone involved in this project	greatness is a potential within this project greatness is a potential within someone involved in this project
Event	"x" is a potential within this event "x" is a potential within someone involved in this event	greatness is a potential within this event greatness is a potential within someone involved in this event

Stabilizing

Keywords:

balancing, calming, establishing, firming, fixing in place, grounding, ordering, securing, settling, smoothing, solidifying, steadying

Description:

A stabilizing force steadies and calms. It discourages swings from one extreme to the other. Conditions become solid and predictable. A card in stabilizing shows a quality that's balancing for the main subject. You may feel grounded by nature (Empress). You may find peace in some area of your life by moving on (Eight of Cups). Even an unpleasant quality can be stabilizing. Avoiding a difficult decision for a time can sometimes help (Two of Swords).

When change is needed, a stabilizing force can mean stagnation. It can set an unwelcome situation in place or reinforce a dull routine. Overextending can keep you tied to a never-ending round of duties (Ten of Wands). A stabilizing energy can be welcome or not, depending on circumstances.

Reversed:

A lack of something is stabilizing. Its absence is having a steadying effect. A situation may become calmer when an opinionated person leaves (reversed Knight of Swords).

Opposite Position:

disrupting

Flex-spread usage:

To the left of the main subject card in the qualities area.

Table 33. STABILIZING Position by Main Subject Type

If the Main Subject is:	Stabilizing suggests: ("x" = some meaning of the card)	Example – Four of Swords (sample meaning = rest)
Self	"x" is stabilizing me	rest is stabilizing me
Other Person	"x" is stabilizing this other person, from my point of view	rest is stabilizing this other person, from my point of view
Group	"x" is stabilizing the group as a whole	rest is stabilizing the group as a whole
Area of Life	"x" is stabilizing within this area of my life	rest is stabilizing within this area of my life
Time Period	"x" tends to be stabilizing during this time period	rest tends to be stabilizing during this time period
Problem	"x" is stabilizing within this problem "x" is stabilizing someone involved in this problem	rest is stabilizing within this problem rest is stabilizing someone involved in this problem
Choice	"x" is stabilizing when it comes to this choice "x" is stabilizing me when it comes to this choice	rest is stabilizing when it comes to this choice rest is stabilizing me when it comes to this choice
Project/Task	"x" is stabilizing within this project "x" is stabilizing someone involved in this project	rest is stabilizing within this project rest is stabilizing someone involved in this project
Event	"x" is stabilizing within this event "x" is stabilizing someone involved in this event	rest is stabilizing within this event rest is stabilizing someone involved in this event

Strong

Keywords:

abundant, big, dominant, extensive, extra, influential, large, major, powerful, vital

Description:

There are two dimensions to strong—size and power. A card in strong shows a quality that's abundant or powerful within the main subject. You may have a strong need for sensual pleasure (Nine of Cups). A strong quality can also be dominant. It has extra power and scope for the moment. Someone who's foolhardy (Knight of Wands) may be dominating a situation.

A strong quality is not necessarily mighty in and of itself. It may simply be strongly present. A powerful attention to detail can be evident during some task (Eight of Pentacles). Often we believe what's strong is preferable, but that's not always true. A strong quality can be welcomed or not, but it's not easily dismissed.

Reversed:

A strong lack of something. It's not just slightly missing, it's really not there. When caring for others, you may lack even a moment to go within yourself (reversed Four of Cups).

Opposite Position:

weak

Flex-spread usage:

To the right of the main subject position in the qualities area.

Table 34. STRONG Position by Main Subject Type

If the Main Subject is:	Strong suggests: ("x" = some meaning of the card)	Example – Nine of Swords (sample meaning = guilt)
Self	"x" is strong within me	guilt is strong within me
Other Person	"x" is strong within this other person, from my point of view	guilt is strong within this other person, from my point of view
Group	"x" is strong within the group as a whole	guilt is strong within the group as a whole
Area of Life	"x" is strong within this area of my life	guilt is strong within this area of my life
Time Period	"x" tends to be strong during this time period	guilt tends to be strong during this time period
Problem	"x" is strong within this problem "x" is strong within someone involved in this problem	guilt is strong within this problem guilt is strong within someone involved in this problem
Choice	"x" is strong when it comes to this choice "x" is strong within me when it comes to this choice	guilt is strong when it comes to this choice guilt is strong within me when it comes to this choice
Project/Task	"x" is strong within this project "x" is strong within someone involved in this project	guilt is strong within this project guilt is strong within someone involved in this project
Event	"x" is strong within this event "x" is strong within someone involved in this event	guilt is strong within this event guilt is strong within someone involved in this event

Temporary

Keywords:

brief, ephemeral, flash-in-the-pan, fleeting, impermanent, interim, momentary, passing, provisional, short-lived, transient, transitory

Description:

Temporary means short-term or provisional. A card in temporary shows a quality that's not expected to last for the main subject. Sometimes, a stop-gap measure is in place, but only until a permanent solution can be found. When you're shorthanded at work, you have to rely on yourself until you can get help (Nine of Pentacles). Quick action may be necessary for a time, but not forever (Eight of Wands).

Sometimes, you can hope something will last, but find out it's only temporary. A task may have been fun for a time, but turned into work (Two of Pentacles). A temporary quality always seems transitory. You know conditions are going to change. Sometimes you're glad a situation is short-term; sometimes you want it to endure.

Reversed:

A temporary lack of something. It's missing for now, but should become available again. You may lack cheer after a poor performance, but know your bad mood will lift (reversed Queen of Wands).

Opposite Position:

enduring

Flex-spread usage:

To the right of the main subject position in the qualities area.

Table 35. TEMPORARY Position by Main Subject Type

If the Main Subject is:	Temporary suggests: ("x" = some meaning of the card)	Example – King of Wands (sample meaning = being bold)
Self	"x" is temporary for me	being bold is temporary for me
Other Person	"x" is temporary for this other person, from my point of view	being bold is temporary for this other person, from my point of view
Group	"x" is temporary for the group as a whole	being bold is temporary for the group as a whole
Area of Life	"x" is temporary within this area of my life	being bold is temporary within this area of my life
Time Period	"x" tends to be temporary during this time period	being bold tends to be temporary during this time period
Problem	"x" is temporary within this problem "x" is temporary for someone involved in this problem	being bold is temporary within this problem being bold is temporary for someone involved in this problem
Choice	"x" is temporary when it comes to this choice "x" is temporary for me when it comes to this choice	being bold is temporary when it comes to this choice being bold is temporary for me when it comes to this choice
Project/Task	"x" is temporary within this project "x" is temporary for someone involved in this project	being bold is temporary within this project being bold is temporary for someone involved with this project
Event	"x" is temporary within this event "x" is temporary for someone involved in this event	being bold is temporary within this event being bold is temporary for someone involved with this event

Unknown

Keywords:

blind to, hidden, in the dark, mysterious, secret, unacquainted with, unaware of, unconscious of, unfamiliar, unrealized, unrecognized, unsuspected

Description:

The unknown is secret and mysterious. It lies hidden or unexposed. The unknown can be something of which the main subject is not yet aware. You may be unaware of a defensive attitude (Nine of Wands). A group may not know a reversal has taken place (Hanged Man).

An unknown quality can also be something rarely, if ever, experienced. It's so unfamiliar as to be unknown. In this sense, serenity may be unheard of among family members or neighbors (Star).

Sometimes the unknown is simply strange and baffling. You don't understand it. You may not yet know the meaning of a fateful moment or personal vision (Wheel of Fortune). It's unknown to you in the deepest sense.

Reversed:

A lack of something is unknown. The main subject may be unaware it's missing or never have gone without it. You may be unaware of a lack of planning on a project (reversed Three of Pentacles).

Opposite Position:

known

Flex-spread usage:

To the left of the main subject position in the qualities area.

Table 36. UNKNOWN Position by Main Subject Type

If the Main Subject is:	Unknown suggests: ("x" = some meaning of the card)	Example – Ten of Wands (sample meaning = struggle)
Self	I don't know "x" "x" is unknown about me	I don't know about struggling my struggle is unknown
Other Person	this other person doesn't know "x," from my point of view "x" is unknown about this person, from my point of view	this other person doesn't know about struggling, from my point of view this other person's struggle is unknown, from my point of view
Group	the group doesn't know "x" "x" is unknown about the group	the group doesn't know about struggling the group's struggle is unknown
Area of Life	I don't know "x" within this area of my life "x" is unknown about this area of my life	I don't know about struggling within this area of my life the struggle within this area of my life is unknown
Time Period	"x" tends to be unknown during this time period	struggling tends to be unknown during this time period
Problem	"x" is unknown within this problem someone involved in this problem doesn't know about "x" "x" is unknown about someone involved in this problem	struggling is unknown within this problem someone involved in this problem doesn't know about struggling the struggle of someone involved in this problem is unknown
Choice	"x" is unknown when it comes to this choice I don't know about "x" when it comes to this choice "x" is unknown about me when it comes to this choice	struggling is unknown when it comes to this choice I don't know about struggling when it comes to this choice my struggle is unknown when it comes to this choice

Table 36. UNKNOWN Position by Main Subject Type, cont.

Project/Task	"x" is unknown within this project	struggling is unknown within this project
	someone involved in this project doesn't know about "x"	someone involved in this project doesn't know about struggling
	"x" is unknown about someone involved in this project	the struggle of someone involved in this project is unknown
Event	"x" is unknown within this event	struggling is unknown within this event
	someone involved in this event doesn't know about "x"	someone involved in this event doesn't know about struggling
	"x" is unknown about someone involved in this event	the struggle of someone involved in this event is unknown

Weak

Keywords:

debilitated, incapacitated, ineffectual, in short supply, limited, low, meager, minor, powerless, reduced, scant, small, subordinate

Description:

Weakness has a negative connotation because we tend to admire strength. But a card in this position doesn't necessarily show something inferior. It simply points out a quality that's reduced for the main subject. It's less available. You may be feeling less of a victim (Ten of Swords). Someone involved in a situation may be less temperamental (Knight of Cups)—this quality is weak.

Sometimes, weak shows something with little power or endurance. A weak relationship (Lovers) may be low on staying power despite efforts to save it. A weak quality may also be little in evidence. A group can be weak in the area of competence (Three of Pentacles). Weakness can be valued or not, depending on circumstances.

Reversed:

A mild lack of something. The absence itself is weak. You may lack good health at the moment, but the ailment is not serious (reversed Temperance).

Opposite Position:

strong

Flex-spread usage:

To the left of the main subject position in the qualities area.

Table 37. WEAK Position by Main Subject Type

If the Main Subject is:	Weak suggests: ("x" = some meaning of the card)	Example – Star (sample meaning = hope)
Self	"x" is weak within me	hope is weak within me
Other Person	"x" is weak within this other person, from my point of view	hope is weak within this other person, from my point of view
Group	"x" is weak within the group as a whole	hope is weak within the group as a whole
Area of Life	"x" is weak within this area of my life	hope is weak within this area of my life
Time Period	"x" tends to be weak during this time period	hope tends to be weak during this time period
Problem	"x" is weak within this problem	hope is weak within this problem
	"x" is weak within someone involved in this problem	hope is weak within someone involved in this problem
Choice	"x" is weak when it comes to this choice	hope is weak when it comes to this choice
	"x" is weak within me when it comes to this choice	hope is weak within me when it comes to this choice
Project/Task	"x" is weak within this project	hope is weak within this project
	"x" is weak within someone involved in this project	hope is weak within someone involved in this project
Event	"x" is weak within this event	hope is weak within this event
	"x" is weak within someone involved in this event	hope is weak within someone involved in this event

SAMPLE FLEX-SPREAD LAYOUTS

This section contains many sample flex-spread layouts. There are layouts for one main subject and for multiple main subjects. At the end are a few layouts useful when doing readings for another person.

Layouts with one main subject

Figure 18. This layout has just one main subject position. It's useful for a quick look at any topic.

Figure 20 (a–f, below and page 144). These layouts are for one main subject (card 1) with no other cards except related people. Related people go below the main subject in horizontal lines, three to a line. If there's a potential person (dotted line), place it in the rightmost position, spaced a little apart. A potential person is placed last among related people.

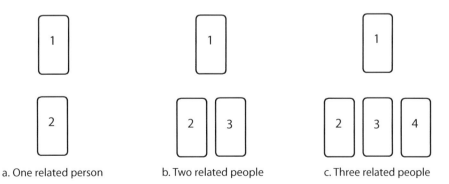

a. One related person   b. Two related people   c. Three related people

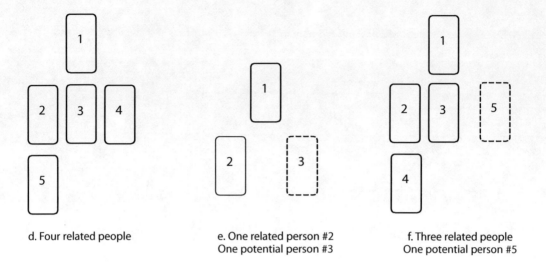

d. Four related people

e. One related person #2
One potential person #3

f. Three related people
One potential person #5

Figure 21 (a–e, below). These layouts are for one main subject (#I), with no other cards except related areas of life. The related areas go to the left of the main subject in vertical lines, two to a line. There's no potential area-of-life position.

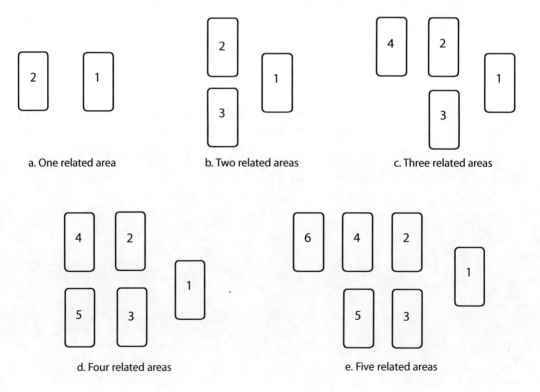

a. One related area

b. Two related areas

c. Three related areas

d. Four related areas

e. Five related areas

Figure 22 (a–f). These layouts are for one main subject (#1), with no other cards except related situations. Related situations go above the main subject in horizontal lines, three to a line. If there's a potential situation (dotted line), place it in the rightmost position, spaced a little apart. A potential situation is placed last among related situations.

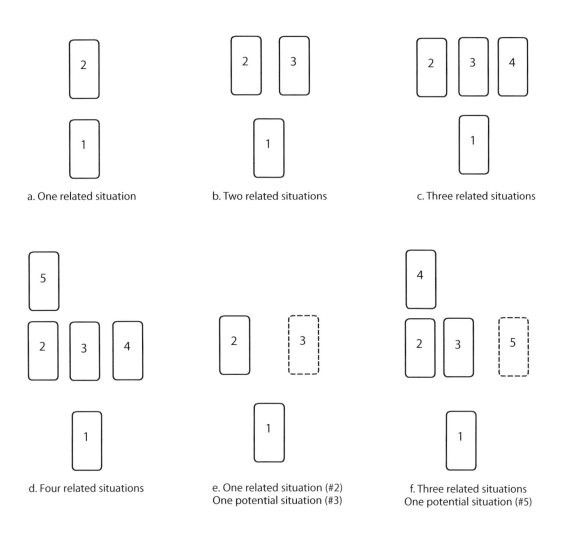

a. One related situation

b. Two related situations

c. Three related situations

d. Four related situations

e. One related situation (#2)
One potential situation (#3)

f. Three related situations
One potential situation (#5)

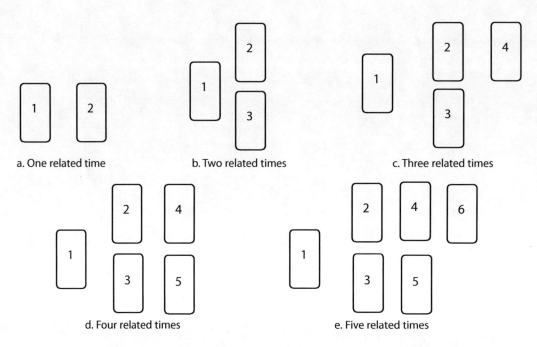

a. One related time

b. Two related times

c. Three related times

d. Four related times

e. Five related times

Figure 23 (a–e, above). These layouts are for one main subject (#I), with no other cards except related time periods. The related time periods go to the right of the main subject in vertical lines, two to a line. There's no potential time period position.

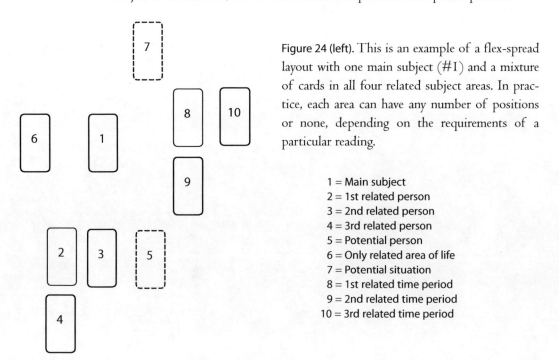

Figure 24 (left). This is an example of a flex-spread layout with one main subject (#I) and a mixture of cards in all four related subject areas. In practice, each area can have any number of positions or none, depending on the requirements of a particular reading.

1 = Main subject
2 = 1st related person
3 = 2nd related person
4 = 3rd related person
5 = Potential person
6 = Only related area of life
7 = Potential situation
8 = 1st related time period
9 = 2nd related time period
10 = 3rd related time period

Figure 25 (a–d). These layouts are for one main subject (#1), with no other cards except qualities. The quality cards are grouped in a rough circle as close to the main subject as possible. Qualities are mainly used in pairs, so the number of positions is even. The order of placement starts at the top and alternates left-right until all quality positions have been placed. Each quality is opposite its pair.

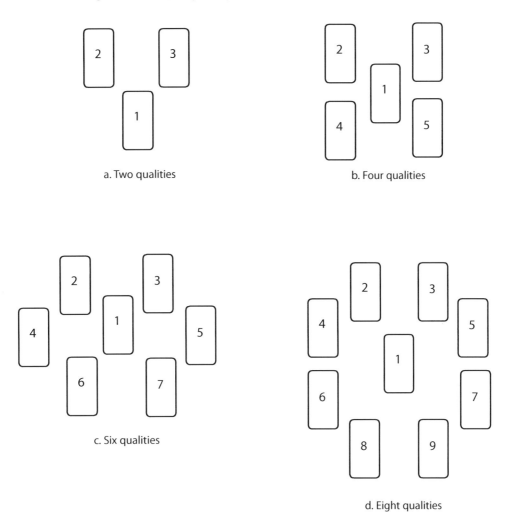

a. Two qualities

b. Four qualities

c. Six qualities

d. Eight qualities

Figure 26 (a–b). Figure 26a shows one main subject (card #1) with four quality pairs, plus the environment and potential quality positions. These two positions have permanent locations above and below the main subject as shown. If they aren't included for a particular reading, these locations are left empty. Figure 26b shows how the environment and potential quality positions work with fewer cards.

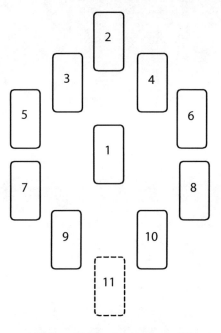

a. Eight qualities + environment (#2)
+ potential quality (#11)

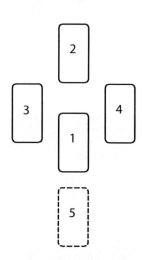

b. Two qualities + environment (#2)
+ potential quality (#5)

Figure 27. This is an example of a flex-spread layout with one main subject (#1) and a mixture of quality and related subject cards in all areas. In practice, each area can have any number of positions or none, depending on the requirements of a particular reading. The two potential related subjects (#15 and #20) are placed slightly apart.

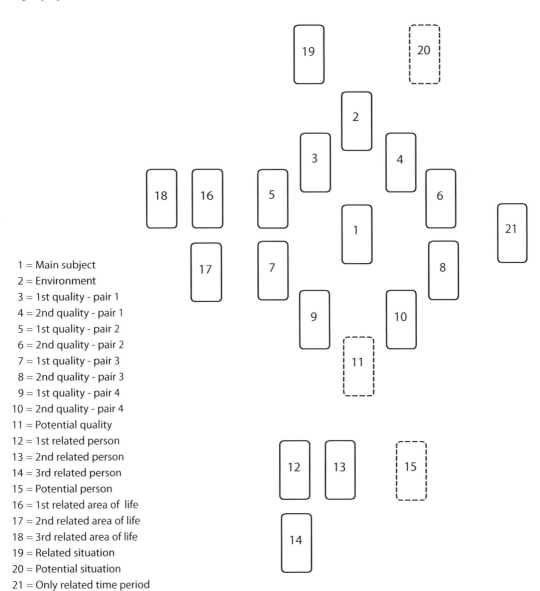

1 = Main subject
2 = Environment
3 = 1st quality - pair 1
4 = 2nd quality - pair 1
5 = 1st quality - pair 2
6 = 2nd quality - pair 2
7 = 1st quality - pair 3
8 = 2nd quality - pair 3
9 = 1st quality - pair 4
10 = 2nd quality - pair 4
11 = Potential quality
12 = 1st related person
13 = 2nd related person
14 = 3rd related person
15 = Potential person
16 = 1st related area of life
17 = 2nd related area of life
18 = 3rd related area of life
19 = Related situation
20 = Potential situation
21 = Only related time period

Figure 29 (a–c). These are three sample layouts with two main subjects with supporting cards. Each main subject is the center of its own set of positions. All cards
are placed for the first main subject, then all for the second, etc. Figure 29a shows
two main subjects with qualities only. Figure 29b has only related people. Figure
29c has a mixture of elements. Multi-subject layouts work best when the position
sets are duplicated for each main subject.

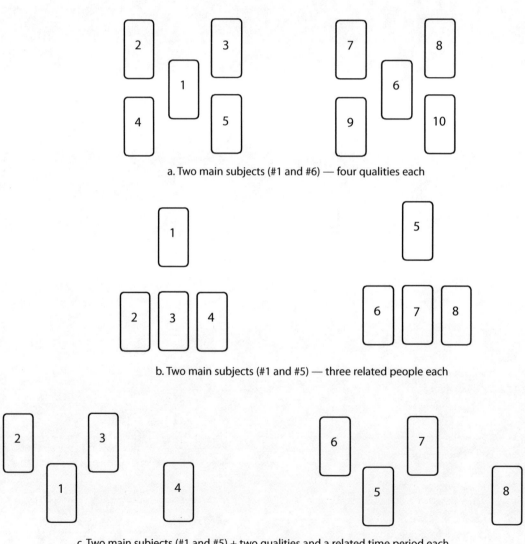

a. Two main subjects (#1 and #6) — four qualities each

b. Two main subjects (#1 and #5) — three related people each

c. Two main subjects (#1 and #5) + two qualities and a related time period each

Sample of Small Layouts - Readings for Others

Figure 30 (a–e). These five small layouts are useful when reading for others. They offer a variety of areas to explore. Multiple-main-subject layouts also work well if they're kept simple.

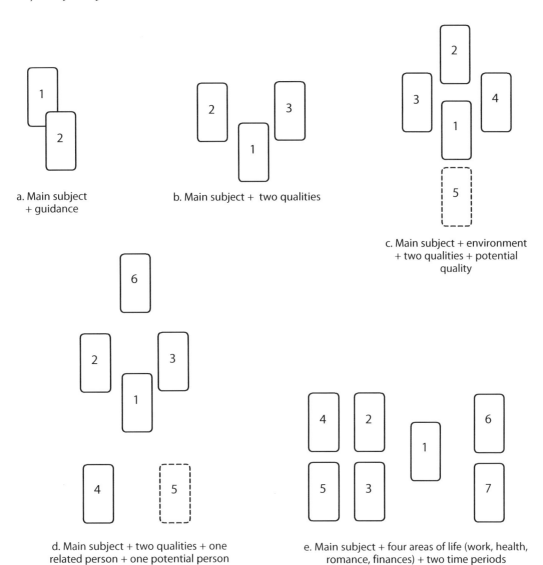

a. Main subject
   + guidance

b. Main subject + two qualities

c. Main subject + environment
   + two qualities + potential
   quality

d. Main subject + two qualities + one
   related person + one potential person
   + one related situation

e. Main subject + four areas of life (work, health,
   romance, finances) + two time periods
   (past and future)

Figure 31. This sample layout is useful for a detailed reading for another person. It includes a variety of qualities and related subjects for a comprehensive overview of the seeker's life at the time of the reading.

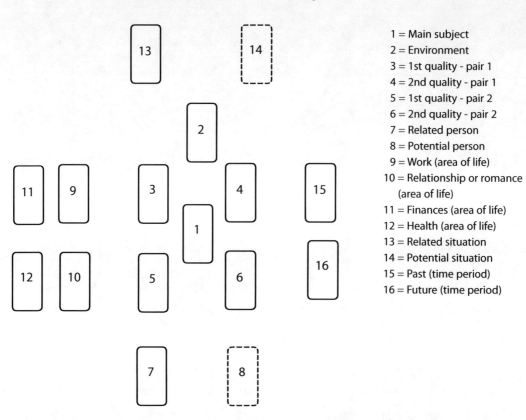

1 = Main subject
2 = Environment
3 = 1st quality - pair 1
4 = 2nd quality - pair 1
5 = 1st quality - pair 2
6 = 2nd quality - pair 2
7 = Related person
8 = Potential person
9 = Work (area of life)
10 = Relationship or romance
    (area of life)
11 = Finances (area of life)
12 = Health (area of life)
13 = Related situation
14 = Potential situation
15 = Past (time period)
16 = Future (time period)

SPREAD SHAPES

This section on pages 154 through 160 contains many sample traditional spread patterns organized by number of cards. The smaller layouts have names. The spreads in this section are not part of the flex-spread system.

Spread Shapes: One-Three Cards

ONE CARD

TWO CARDS

Horizontal   Vertical   Ascending   Descending   Stacked

THREE CARDS

Horizontal   Vertical   Ascending   Descending

Triangle   Inverted Triangle   Stacked with Single

Spread Shapes: Four Cards

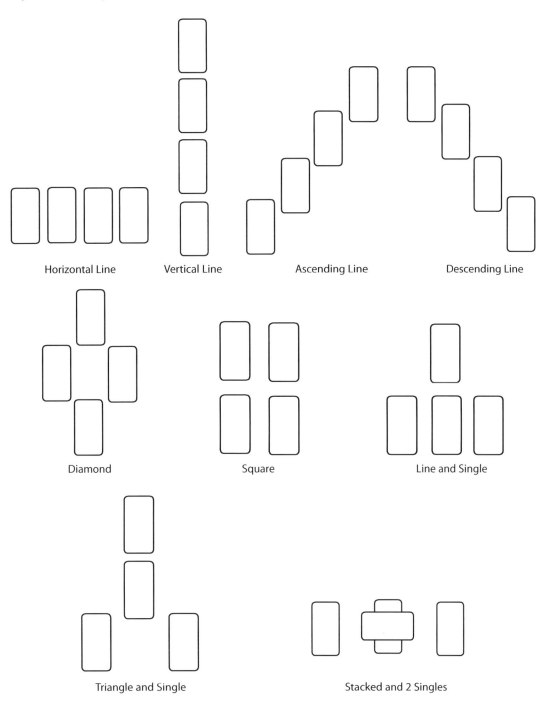

Horizontal Line   Vertical Line   Ascending Line   Descending Line

Diamond   Square   Line and Single

Triangle and Single   Stacked and 2 Singles

Spread Shapes: Five Cards

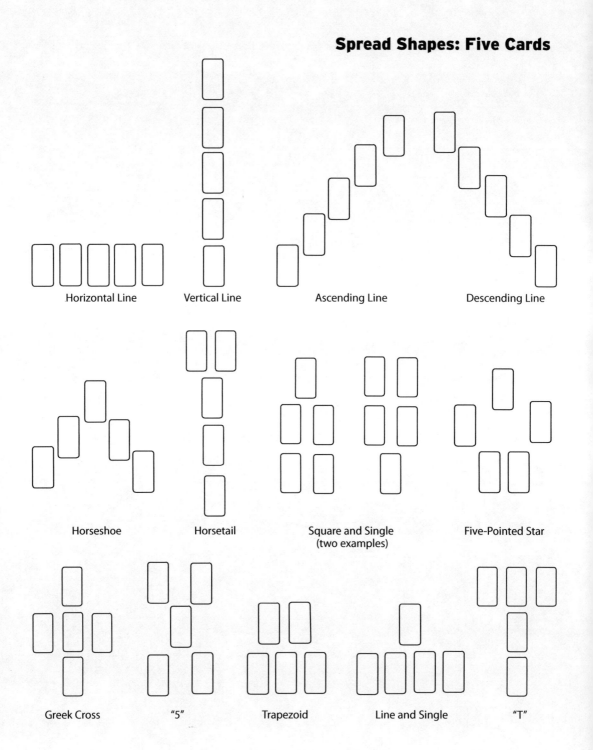

Horizontal Line Vertical Line Ascending Line Descending Line

Horseshoe Horsetail Square and Single (two examples) Five-Pointed Star

Greek Cross "5" Trapezoid Line and Single "T"

Spread Shapes: Six Cards

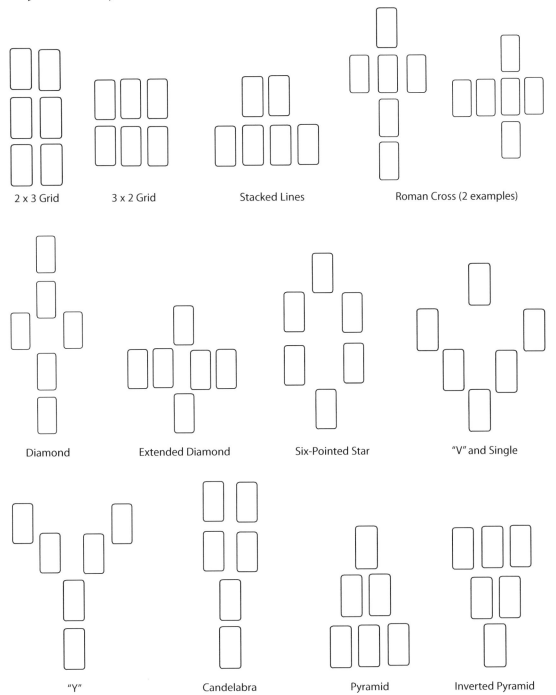

2 x 3 Grid

3 x 2 Grid

Stacked Lines

Roman Cross (2 examples)

Diamond

Extended Diamond

Six-Pointed Star

"V" and Single

"Y"

Candelabra

Pyramid

Inverted Pyramid

Spread Shapes: Seven+ Cards

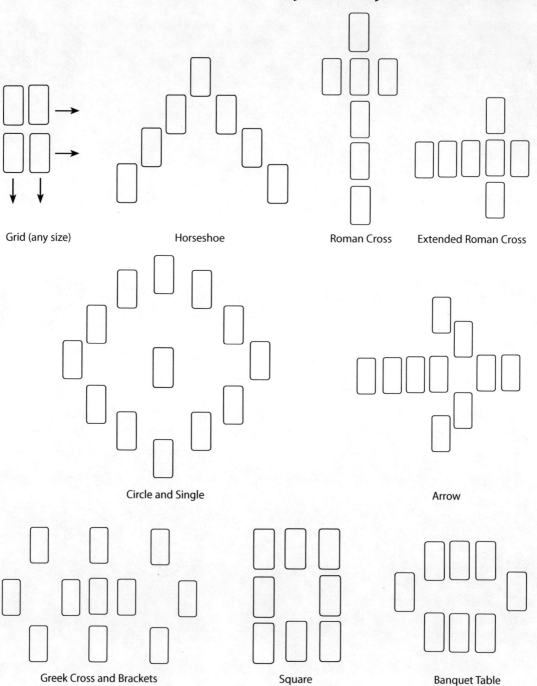

Grid (any size)   Horseshoe   Roman Cross   Extended Roman Cross

Circle and Single   Arrow

Greek Cross and Brackets   Square   Banquet Table

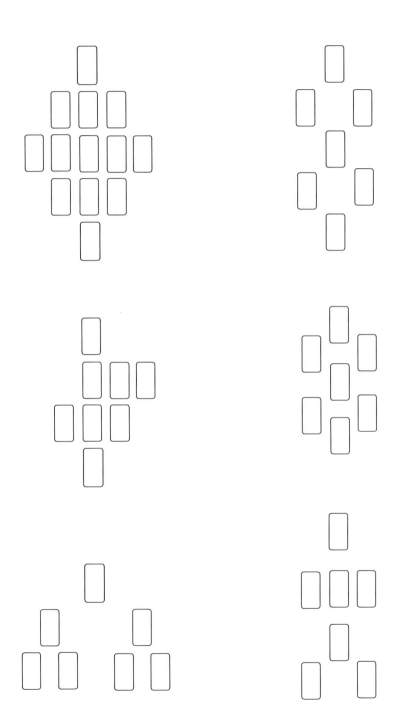

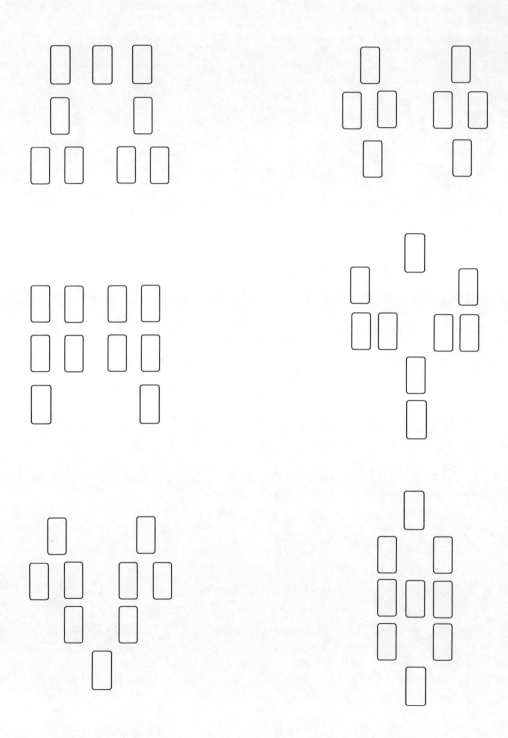

APPENDIX A:

EXERCISE ANSWER KEY

Here are possible answers to some of the exercises. Don't be concerned if your answers are different. These are my suggestions only.

Positions in Your Favorite Spreads (see exercise 2, page 14)

My matches for the Celtic Cross Spread are:

> Celtic Cross position 1—main subject
> Celtic Cross position 2—none, or possibly related subject
> Celtic Cross position 3—unknown quality
> Celtic Cross position 4—related time period (past)
> Celtic Cross position 5—known quality
> Celtic Cross position 6—related time period (future)
> Celtic Cross position 7—related person (self)
> Celtic Cross position 8—environment
> Celtic Cross position 9—guidance
> Celtic Cross position 10—heading toward

Choosing Single or Multiple Main Subjects (see exercise 1, page 57)

1. Single—*me* (self), *my life* (area of life), or *the present* (time period)
2. Single— *upcoming concert* (event)
3. Multiple— *yes* and *no* (choices)
4. Single— *my health* (area of life), or *being tired all the time* (problem)
5. Multiple— *team 1, team 2* and *team 3* (groups)
6. Multiple— *grandchild 1* and *grandchild 2* (other people)
7. Single— *problem with my dog* (problem)
8. Single— *past* (time period)
9. Single— *my depression* (area of life or problem)
10. Multiple— *project 1, project 2, project 3* and *project 4* (projects)

Layout Design Practice (exercise 2, page 57)

Scenario 1

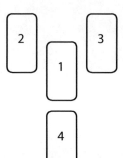

I = self
2 = my diet (area of life)

Scenario 2

1 = my finances (area of life)
2 = enduring
3 = temporary
4 = potential quality

Scenario 3

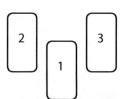

I = moving to Chicago
(choice I)
2 = old 3 = new

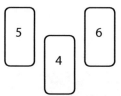

4 = moving to DC
(choice 2)
5 = old 6 = new

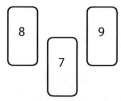

7 = moving to Boston
(choice 3)
8 = old 9 = new

Scenario 4

I = book project
2 = avoiding
3 = embracing
4 = potential situation

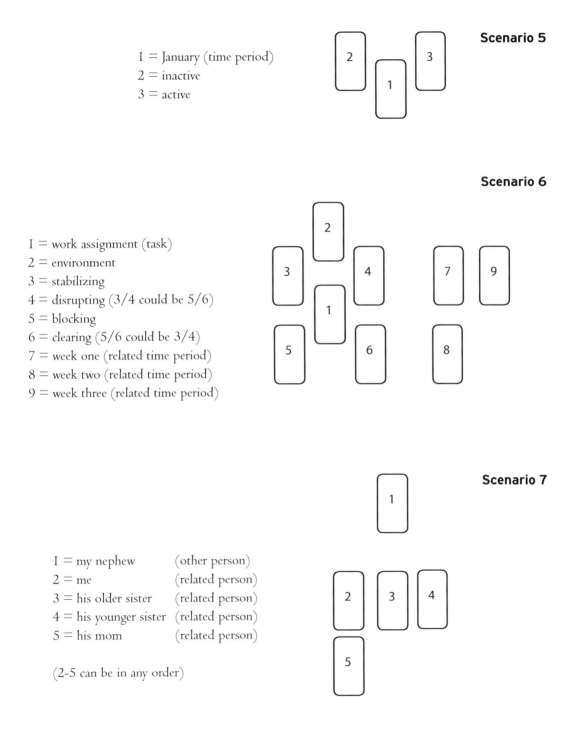

Scenario 5

1 = January (time period)
2 = inactive
3 = active

Scenario 6

1 = work assignment (task)
2 = environment
3 = stabilizing
4 = disrupting (3/4 could be 5/6)
5 = blocking
6 = clearing (5/6 could be 3/4)
7 = week one (related time period)
8 = week two (related time period)
9 = week three (related time period)

Scenario 7

1 = my nephew   (other person)
2 = me   (related person)
3 = his older sister   (related person)
4 = his younger sister (related person)
5 = his mom   (related person)

(2-5 can be in any order)

Scenario 8

1 = fight with John (problem)
2 = contributing to
3 = moving forward
4 = me (related person)
5 = John (related person)
6 = our relationship (related area of life)
7 = last month's fight (related situation)

Scenario 9

1 = class one
2 = class two
3 = class three
4 = class four
(all main subjects)

Scenario 10

1 = self
2 = weak
3 = strong
4 = my partner (related person)
5 = my health (related area of life)

Valid Serial Reading Choices for Scenarios 1-10
(see exercise 1, page 61)

1. my diet—a related area of life
2. none—all are qualities
3. none—because there are quality cards for the subject choices already
4. potential situation—the only related subject
5. none—only qualities
6. week one, week two, week three, week four—the only related subjects
7. his older sister, his younger sister, his mom, me—all related people
8. John, me, our relationship, last month's fight—all related subjects
9. class 1, class 2, class 3, class 4—main subjects with no detail cards as yet
10. my health, my partner—the two related subjects

APPENDIX B:

AREAS OF LIFE AND TIME PERIODS

AREAS OF LIFE

Career
    Job
    Vocation
Community
    Neighborhood
Creative Expression
    Talent
Family Life
Finances
    Investments
    Money
Friendships
Health
    Body
    Physical Condition
    Diet
    Exercise
Hobby or Pastime
Marriage or Partnership
Relationship
Romance
Sexuality
Spirituality or Religion
Sports
Volunteer Work

TIME PERIODS

Day
    Hours
    Morning
    Afternoon
    Night
Week
    Days of the Week
    Workdays
    Weekend
Month
    Phases of the Moon
    Weeks
Year
    Astrological Phases
    Spring
    Summer
    Fall
    Winter
    Growing Seasons
    Months
    Quarters

Personal Time Periods
School- or Work-Related
    Breaks or Vacations
    Quarters
    Semesters

Here are some sample keyword meanings for each tarot card. The same keywords are used in *Learning the Tarot.*

MAJOR ARCANA

FOOL (0)	MAGICIAN (1)	HIGH PRIESTESS (2)	EMPRESS (3)
Beginning Spontaneity Faith Apparent Folly	Action Conscious Awareness Concentration Power	Nonaction Unconscious Awareness Potential Mystery	Motherhood Abundance Senses Nature
EMPEROR (4)	**HIEROPHANT (5)**	**LOVERS (6)**	**CHARIOT (7)**
Fatherhood Structure Authority Regulation	Education Belief Systems Conformity Group Identification	Relationship Sexuality Personal Beliefs Values	Victory Will Self-Assertion Hard Control
STRENGTH (8)	**HERMIT (9)**	**WHEEL OF FORTUNE (10)**	**JUSTICE (11)**
Strength Patience Compassion Soft Control	Introspection Searching Guidance Solitude	Destiny Turning Point Movement Personal Vision	Justice Responsibility Decision Cause and Effect
HANGED MAN (12)	**DEATH (13)**	**TEMPERANCE (14)**	**DEVIL (15)**
Letting Go Reversal Suspension Sacrifice	Ending Transition Elimination Inexorable Forces	Temperance Balance Health Combination	Bondage Materialism Ignorance Hopelessness
TOWER (16)	**STAR (17)**	**MOON (18)**	**SUN (19)**
Sudden Change Release Downfall Revelation	Hope Inspiration Generosity Serenity	Fear Illusion Imagination Bewilderment	Enlightenment Greatness Vitality Assurance
	JUDGMENT (20)	**WORLD (21)**	
	Judgment Rebirth Inner Calling Absolution	Integration Accomplishment Involvement Fulfillment	

MINOR ARCANA—ACE-TEN

	WANDS	CUPS	SWORDS	PENTACLES
ACE	Creative Force Enthusiasm Confidence Courage	Emotional Force Intuition Intimacy Love	Mental Force Truth Justice Fortitude	Material Force Prosperity Practicality Trust
TWO	Personal Power Boldness Originality	Connection Truce Attraction	Blocked Emotions Avoidance Stalemate	Juggling Flexibility Fun
THREE	Exploration Foresight Leadership	Exuberance Friendship Community	Heartbreak Loneliness Betrayal	Teamwork Planning Competence
FOUR	Celebration Freedom Excitement	Self-Absorption Apathy Going Within	Rest Contemplation Quiet Preparation	Possessiveness Control Blocked Change
FIVE	Disagreement Competition Hassles	Loss Bereavement Regret	Self-Interest Discord Open Dishonor	Hard Times Ill Health Rejection
SIX	Triumph Acclaim Pride	Goodwill Innocence Childhood	The Blues Recovery Travel	Having/Not Having: Resources Knowledge Power
SEVEN	Aggression Defiance Conviction	Wishful Thinking Options Dissipation	Running Away Lone-Wolf Style Hidden Dishonor	Assessment Reward Direction Change
EIGHT	Quick Action Conclusion News	Deeper Meaning Moving On Weariness	Restriction Confusion Powerlessness	Diligence Knowledge Detail
NINE	Defensiveness Perseverance Stamina	Wish Fulfillment Satisfaction Sensual Pleasure	Worry Guilt Anguish	Discipline Self-Reliance Refinement
TEN	Overextending Burdens Struggle	Joy Peace Family	Bottoming Out Victim Mentality Martyrdom	Affluence Permanence Convention

MINOR ARCANA-COURT CARDS

	WANDS	CUPS	SWORDS	PENTACLES
PAGE	Be Creative Be Enthusiastic Be Courageous Be Confident	Be Emotional Be Intuitive Be Intimate Be Loving	Use Your Mind Be Truthful Be Just Have Fortitude	Have an Effect Be Practical Be Prosperous Be Trusting/ Trustworthy
KNIGHT Positive	Charming Self-Confident Daring Adventurous Passionate	Romantic Imaginative Sensitive Refined Introspective	Direct Authoritative Incisive Knowledgeable Logical	Unwavering Cautious Thorough Realistic Hardworking
KNIGHT Negative	Superficial Cocky Foolhardy Restless Hot-Tempered	Overemotional Fanciful Temperamental Overrefined Introverted	Blunt Overbearing Cutting Opinionated Unfeeling	Stubborn Unadventurous Obsessive Pessimistic Grinding
QUEEN	Attractive Wholehearted Energetic Cheerful Self-Assured	Loving Tenderhearted Intuitive Psychic Spiritual	Honest Astute Forthright Witty Experienced	Nurturing Bighearted Down-to-Earth Resourceful Trustworthy
KING	Creative Inspiring Forceful Charismatic Bold	Wise Calm Diplomatic Caring Tolerant	Intellectual Analytical Articulate Just Ethical	Enterprising Adept Reliable Supporting Steady

FLEX-SPREAD READING PROCEDURE

These are the steps for a flex-spread reading you do for yourself.[10] Steps with an asterisk (*) are described in detail in *Learning the Tarot*.

1. Prepare yourself and the outer environment. Have on hand your tarot deck, any references, a pen, and notepaper.

2. Clarify the direction you want to go in your reading.

3. Choose one or more main subjects and give each a name. Identify each subject's type.

4. Decide on a layout based on your goals and interests. Review and memorize your layout if you can.

5. Speak an opening statement—any message you wish to say aloud about yourself and the reading.*

6. Shuffle and cut the cards. This is the defining moment, when the energies of the reading are fixed. Have faith in your goal and intentions!*

7. Place the cards according to your layout.

8. Review the cards and their relationships. Look for patterns and oppositions. Let your feelings be your guide. Balance intellectual analysis with intuition. *

9. Write down the chosen cards and make notes.

10. Optional: Select cards for guidance. Tip these cards to confirm your choices.

11. Shuffle and cut the unused deck. Place guidance card(s) in the order of the tipped cards.

---

10 See lesson 12 for a discussion of readings you do for others.

12. Review and interpret. Write down the chosen cards and make notes.

13. Weave a meaningful story from the cards. The story doesn't have to be elaborate. Speak your story out loud.*

14. Write a summary statement—a quick version of your story to use as a guide after the reading is over.*

15. Optional: Select a subject(s) for a serial reading. Place the new main subject in the center. Gather all the rest of the cards. Go back to step 4 and continue as before.

16. Do the tasks required to end the reading smoothly. Clear your deck and put it away. Say an ending statement, if you like.*

17. Use your tarot insights to make real, productive changes in your life.

BIBLIOGRAPHY

Abraham, Sylvia. *How to Read the Tarot: The Key Word System.* St Paul, MN: Llewellyn, 1994.

———. *How to Use Tarot Spreads: Answers to Every Question.* St. Paul, MN: Llewellyn, 1997.

Almond, Jocelyn, and Keith Seddon. *Understanding Tarot: A Practical Guide to Tarot Card Reading.* London: Aquarian, 1991.

Amaral, Geraldine, and Nancy Brady Cunningham. *Tarot Celebrations: Honoring the Inner Voice.* York, ME: Samuel Weiser, 1997.

Amberstone, Ruth Ann, and Wald Amberstone. *Tarot Tips.* St. Paul: Llewellyn, 2003.

Anonymous. *Meditations on the Tarot: A Journey into Christian Hermeticism.* Rockport, MA: Element, 1985.

Aviza, Edward A. *Thinking Tarot.* New York: Fireside, 1997.

Banzhaf, Hajo. *Tarot and the Journey of the Hero.* Boston, MA: Samuel Weiser, 2000.

———. *The Tarot Handbook.* Stamford, CT: U. S. Games, 1993.

Banzhaf, Hajo, and Elisa Hemmerlein. *Tarot as Your Companion: A Practical Guide to the Rider-Waite and Crowley Thoth Tarot Decks.* Stamford, CT: U. S. Games, 1999.

Banzhaf, Hajo, and Elisa Hemmerlein. *Tarot as Your Companion: A Practical Guide to the Rider-Waite and Crowley Thoth Tarot Decks.* Stamford, CT: U. S. Games, 1999.

Berres, Janet. *Textbook of the Tarot.* Morton Grove, IL: International Tarot Society, 1990.

Braden, Nina Lee. *Tarot for Self-Discovery.* St. Paul: Llewellyn, 2002.

Burger, Evelin, and Johannes Fiebig. *Complete Book of Tarot Spreads.* New York: Sterling, 1995.

Clarson, Laura E. *Tarot Unveiled: The Method to Its Magic.* Stamford, CT: U. S. Games, 2002.

Connolly, Eileen. *Tarot: A New Handbook for the Apprentice.* North Hollywood, CA: Newcastle, 1979.

———. *Tarot: A New Handbook for the Journeyman.* North Hollywood, CA: Newcastle, 1987.

Cortellesi, Linda. *The User-Friendly Tarot Guidebook.* Worthington, OH: Chalice Moon Publications, 1996.

Cowie, Norma. *Tarot for Successful Living.* White Rock, Canada: NC Publishing, 1979.

D'Agostino, Joseph D. *Tarot: The Royal Path to Wisdom.* York, ME: Samuel Weiser, 1976.

Decker, Ronald, and Michael Dummett. *A History of the Occult Tarot: 1870–1970.* London: Duckworth, 2002.

Denning, Melita, and Osborne Phillips. *The Magick of the Tarot.* St. Paul, MN: Llewellyn, 1983.

Doane, Doris Chase, and King Keyes. *How to Read Tarot Cards.* New York: Barnes & Noble, 1967.

Echols, Signe E., Robert Mueller, and Sandra A. Thomson. *Spiritual Tarot: Seventy-Eight Paths to Personal Development.* New York: Avon, 1996.

Fairfield, Gail. *Choice-Centered Relating and the Tarot.* Boston, MA: Samuel Weiser, 2000.

———. *Choice Centered Tarot.* North Hollywood, CA: Newcastle, 1984.

Galenorn, Yasmine. *Tarot Journeys: Adventures in Self-Transformation.* St. Paul, MN: Llewellyn, 1999.

Garen, Nancy. *Creating Your Own Tarot Cards.* New York: Fireside, 1991.

———. *Tarot Made Easy.* New York: Fireside, 1989.

Gerulskis-Estes, Susan. *The Book of Tarot.* Dobbs Ferry, NY: Morgan & Morgan, 1981.

Giles, Cynthia. *The Tarot: History, Mystery, and Lore.* New York: Fireside, 1992.

Gillentine, Julie. *Tarot & Dream Interpretation.* St. Paul, MN: Llewellyn, 2003.

Graves, F. D. *The Windows of Tarot.* Dobbs Ferry, NY: Morgan & Morgan, 1973.

Gray, Eden. *A Complete Guide to the Tarot.* New York: Bantam, 1970.

———. *Mastering the Tarot: Basic Lessons in an Ancient, Mystic Art.* New York: New American Library, 1971.

———. *The Tarot Revealed.* New York: New American Library, 1960.

Greer, Mary K. *The Complete Book of Tarot Reversals.* St. Paul, MN: Llewellyn, 2002.

———. *Tarot for Yourself: A Workbook for Personal Transformation.* North Hollywood, CA: Newcastle, 1984.

Greer, Mary K., and Rachel Pollack, eds. *New Thoughts on Tarot.* North Hollywood, CA: Newcastle, 1989.

Greer, Mary K., and Tom Little. *Understanding the Tarot Court.* St. Paul, MN: Llewellyn, 2004.

Gregory, James. *How to Perform a Psychic Reading: A Beginner's Guide to Reading Tarot Cards.* Colorado Springs, CO: Zymore Press, 1999.

Haga, Enoch. *TARO Solution: A Complete Guide to Interpreting the Tarot.* Livermore, CA: Enoch Haga Publisher, 1994.

Hamaker-Zondag, Karen. *Tarot as a Way of Life: A Jungian Approach to the Tarot.* York, ME: Samuel Weiser, 1997.

Hazel, Elizabeth. *Tarot Decoded: Understanding and Using Dignities and Correspondences.* Boston, MA: Weiser Books, 2004.

Hollander, P. Scott. *Tarot for Beginners.* St. Paul, MN: Llewellyn, 1995.

Irwin, Lee. *Gnostic Tarot: Mandalas for Spiritual Transformation.* York, ME: Samuel Weiser, 1998.

Jette, Christine. *Professional Tarot: The Business of Reading, Consulting & Teaching.* St. Paul, MN: Llewellyn, 2003.

———. *Tarot for All Seasons.* St. Paul, MN: Llewellyn, 2001.

———. *Tarot for the Healing Heart: Using Inner Wisdom to Heal Body and Mind.* St. Paul, MN: Llewellyn, 2001.

———. *Tarot Shadow Work: Using the Dark Symbols to Heal.* St. Paul, MN: Llewellyn, 2001.

Junjulas, Craig. *Psychic Tarot.* Stamford, CT: U. S. Games, 1985.

K, Amber, and Azrael Arynn K. *Heart of Tarot: An Intuitive Approach.* St. Paul, MN: Llewellyn, 2002.

Kaplan, Stuart R. *The Encyclopedia of Tarot: Volumes 1–3.* Stamford, CT: U. S. Games, 1978, 1986, 1990.

———. *Tarot Cards for Fun and Fortune Telling.* Stamford, CT: U. S. Games, 1970.

Kaser, R. T. *Tarot in Ten Minutes.* New York: Avon, 1992.

Kelly, Dorothy. *Tarot Card Combinations.* Boston, MA: Weiser Books, 2003.

Knight, Gareth. *The Magical World of the Tarot: Fourfold Mirror of the Universe.* York, ME: Samuel Weiser, 1991.

Konraad, Sandor. *Classic Tarot Spreads.* Atglen, PA: Whitford Press, 1985.

Louis, Anthony. *Tarot Plain and Simple.* St. Paul, MN: Llewellyn, 1997.

MacGregor, Trish, and Phyllis Vega. *Power Tarot.* New York: Fireside, 1998.

Masino, Marcia. *Easy Tarot Guide.* San Diego, CA: ACS Publications, 1987.

McElroy, Mark. *Putting the Tarot to Work.* St. Paul, MN: Llewellyn, 2004.

Michelsen, Teresa. *Designing Your Own Tarot Spreads.* St. Paul, MN: Llewellyn, 2003.

Moura, Ann. *Tarot for the Green Witch.* St. Paul, MN: Llewellyn, 2003.

Nichols, Sallie. *Jung and Tarot: An Archetypal Journey.* York, ME: Samuel Weiser, 1980.

Oken, Alan. *Pocket Guide to the Tarot.* Berkeley, CA: Crossing Press, 1996.

Peach, Emily. *The Tarot Workbook: Understanding and Using Tarot Symbolism.* New York: Sterling, 1990.

Pielmeier, Heidemarie, and Marcus Schirner. *Illustrated Tarot Spreads: 78 New Layouts for Personal Discovery.* New York: Sterling, 1999.

Pollack, Rachel. *Complete Illustrated Guide to Tarot: How to Unlock the Secrets of the Tarot.* New York: Gramercy Books, 1999.

———. *The Forest of Souls: A Walk through the Tarot.* St. Paul, MN: Llewellyn, 2002.

———. *Seventy-Eight Degrees of Wisdom: A Book of Tarot, Part 1: The Major Arcana.* London: Aquarian, 1980.

———. *Seventy-Eight Degrees of Wisdom: A Book of Tarot, Part 2: The Minor Arcana and Readings.* London: Aquarian, 1980.

Porter, Tracy. *Tarot Companion: An Essential Reference Guide.* St. Paul, MN: Llewellyn, 2000.

Prosapio, Richard, with Elizabeth Prosapio. *Intuitive Tarot: Discovering the Power of Your Intuition.* Stamford, CT: U. S. Games, 1996.

Renee, Janina. *Tarot for a New Generation.* St. Paul, MN: Llewellyn, 2002.

———. *Tarot Spells.* St. Paul, MN: Llewellyn, 1990 and 2000.

———. *Tarot: Your Everyday Guide.* St. Paul, MN: Llewellyn, 2000.

Ricklef, James. *Tarot Tells the Tale: Explore Three-Card Readings through Familiar Stories.* St. Paul, MN: Llewellyn, 2003.

Riley, Jana. *Tarot: Dictionary and Compendium.* York, ME: Samuel Weiser, 1995.

Rosengarten, Arthur. *Tarot and Psychology: Spectrums of Possibility.* St. Paul, MN: Paragon House, 2000.

Sharman-Burke, Juliet. *The Complete Book of Tarot: A Step-by-Step Guide to Reading the Cards.* New York: St. Martin's, 1985.

———. *Understanding the Tarot: A Personal Teaching Guide.* New York: St. Martin's, 1998.

Shavick, Nancy. *The Tarot Reader.* New York: Berkley, 1991.

Simon, Sylvie. *The Tarot: Art, Mysticism, Divination.* Rochester, VT: Inner Traditions, 1986.

Sterling, Stephen Walter. *Tarot Awareness: Exploring the Spiritual Path.* St. Paul, MN: Llewellyn, 2000.

Townley, Kevin. *The Cube of Space; Container of Creation.* Boulder, CO: Archive Press, 1993.

Vega, Phyllis. *Romancing the Tarot.* New York: Fireside, 2001.

Waite, Arthur Edward. *Pictorial Key to the Tarot.* York, ME: Samuel Weiser, 1993.

Wang, Robert. *Qabalistic Tarot.* York, ME: Samuel Weiser, 1983.

Wanless, James. *New Age Tarot: A Workbook and Glossary of Symbols.* Carmel, CA: Merrill-West Publishing, 1986.

Woudhuysen, Jan. *Tarot Therapy: A New Approach to Self Exploration.* Los Angeles: Jeremy P. Tarcher, 1979.

ABOUT THE AUTHOR

Joan Bunning grew up in Washington, DC during the 1950s. She received her B.A. in Social Psychology from Cornell University and has worked as a writer, computer programmer, and Web site developer. In September 1995, Bunning launched the "Learning the Tarot" Web site at *www.learningthetarot.com*. She lives in Virginia with her husband and dog Maggie.

TO OUR READERS

Weiser Books, an imprint of Red Wheel/Weiser, publishes books across the entire spectrum of occult and esoteric subjects. Our mission is to publish quality books that will make a difference in people's lives without advocating any one particular path or field of study. We value the integrity, originality, and depth of knowledge of our authors.

Our readers are our most important resource, and we appreciate your input, suggestions, and ideas about what you would like to see published. Please feel free to contact us, to request our latest book catalog, or to be added to our mailing list.

Red Wheel/Weiser, LLC
500 Third Street, Suite 230
San Francisco, CA 94107
www.redwheelweiser.com